Footprint

Copenhagen

Sean Sheehan

Contents

Listings

About the author

Lured by rumours of libertarian lifestyles, Sean Sheehan hitchhiked to Scandinavia as a student but after a day spent trying to get a lift north from Malmö returned to Copenhagen. Subsequent visits to the Danish capital led to the 'discovery' of Christiania. Sean is the co-author of the Footprint guides to Ireland and Dublin and his most recent book, Anarchism, features Copenhagen. Sean now lives in London and Ireland.

Contributor
Paul Barfoot wrote the Bars and clubs and Arts and entertainment chapter, as well as adding to the Gay and lesbian chapter. Having graduated with an English and Drama degree Paul went to work for the BBC. In 2002 he relocated from London to Copenhagen where he works freelance as a Contributing Editor for several lifestyle and design titles.

Acknowledgements

Sean would like to thank all the people who helped with the research for this guide: Brit Lightbody, Emelie Klein, Katarina Olsson, Jeppe Mühlhausen, Thomas Tholstrup, Marie Trappaud Rønne, Pam Ahluwalia, Claus Olesen, Michael Trixi Nielsen, Aileesh Carew, Peter Jørgensen, Jørgen W Frederiksen, Kirsten Losang, Lotte Wagner, Kristen Windset, Kirsten Glente, and Mate Vucie. Special thanks to Zid in Christiania, and Flemming Lund for extricating me from a late-night transport problem.

Most cities come pre-packed these days and the adjectives that form the lightweight wrapping make unavoidable mental baggage for the independently-minded traveller. Barcelona is sexy and postmodern, Dublin is green and hip, Paris is Paris, and Copenhagen is hmm...? What do we say about the capital of Denmark, the land that gave us lego, lurpak and the snorkel? Saying it is understated chic hardly raises the blood pressure. We know it's Scandinavian and that hints at the sensual and the liberated. An existentialist philosopher called Kierkegaard hailed from the city, and isn't there some statue of a mermaid that keeps getting decapitated? All this is true but it hardly opens a window on the city's soul. Copenhagen, in fact, is a serious contender for Europe's best-kept secret. Surprise is the bonus that comes with a city that is not presented in tourist cellophane.

Low-key glamour

Tour buses disgorging swarms of camera-toting visitors are relatively uncommon. The tourist office brashly naming itself Wonderful Copenhagen is one of the few reminders that your visitor status is being marketed. It is because you rarely feel like a rubberneck that the city opens itself up in surprising ways. Sightseeing becomes a more personal odyssey than in most European capitals and Copenhagen's world-class museums and art galleries, the city's ever-so-literate awareness of architecture and design, and the everyday style and pace of life all become something to be discovered and experienced as new.

Tradition by design

The city's physical face is essential to its style. It is small and so easy to get around. Everyone cycles, pedestrianized areas are common-place, and the legacy of 17th-century planning characterizes much of what is best about the shape and feel of the city. Canals and lakes, parks and palaces, the sombre and muted colours of buildings combine to evoke a sense of historical time that Copenhagen has no intention of relinquishing in the name of progress. Yet alongside this respect for the past and contempt for symbols of modernity, like skyscrapers, there is an eager anticipation for modern design. Architects and designers are household names, and it is not difficult to find hotels and restaurants that are proud – and not in the name-dropping sense – of their designer shower fittings, sofas or lamps.

On the road

Contraries coexist in and around Copenhagen. The medieval quarter of the city is a short bus ride away from the experimental 'free city' of Christiania; the traditional architecture of Malmö in Sweden is reached via Europe's most ultra-modern bridge in little over half an hour; and speedy trains zip up to the North Zealand Coast accessing the ancient castle of Shakespeare's Hamlet; not forgetting one of the world's finest galleries, by the sea, Louisiana.

At a glance

Rådhuspladsen and around

Rådhuspladsen (Town Hall Square) is the Times Square/Piccadilly Circus of Copenhagen, with the famed Tivoli Gardens to the south and the capital's major shopping street, the pedestrianized Strøget (pronounced 'strool'), commencing at its northeast corner. The square is only a stone's throw from Central Station, as well as being home to the city's bus terminus, and given the capital's small size there is no way you won't repeatedly pass across it on journeys to and from somewhere else. But don't let your growing familiarity with the square take the shine off its intrinsic appeal, for Rådhuspladsen reflects the city's character in its Danish grandeur, open access and in the murmur of human traffic; especially when, late in the evening, unobtrusive neon shines down from the surrounding buildings and a shimmer of glitz and modest glamour fills the air. From Strøget, it is a short walk to the old university area of the city.

Slotsholmen and around

To the northeast of Rådhuspladsen, and a 10-minute walk away, lies Slotsholmen. The historical heart of Copenhagen, Slotsholmen is an oblong-shaped island enclosed by narrow canals on three sides and facing the harbour to its south. To defeat Baltic pirates Bishop Absalon built a stone castle here in the 12th century, in a fishing village called Havn or Købmændenes (Merchants' Haven), and the rest is history. On this small island today, there is a cluster of buildings that chart the evolution of the city from the 1167 castle to the contemporary Danish Parliament. Slotsholmen is confusingly compact, a maze of passageways, arches and hidden doors through which visitors wander trying to identify what's what. A stone's throw away, on the other side of the surrounding waterways, there are chic pavement restaurants and cafés where you can recuperate and indulge in some people-watching.

Nyhavn and around

To the north of Slotsholmen, another 10-minutes on foot, is Nyhavn, a pedestrianized street facing a 17th-century canal dug to facilitate commerce. Nyhavn is not only a Mecca for beer-quaffing Swedes – the Malmö ferry is close by – but home to a happy medley of cafés and restaurants spilling onto the pavement, welcoming all and sundry. The canal was built to access Kongens Nytorv, a wide-open, unfilled square of grand proportions dignified by some of the city's most magnificent buildings. This area around the top end of Strøget is the posh end of town, with restaurants, pavement cafés and exclusive stores for the beau monde. To the north and northeast of Nyhavn lies a broad swathe of parks and boulevards that boast royal connections – including Rosenborg Slot and the palaces of Amalienborg – a far cry from the Nyhavn's lively atmosphere of vivacious, but never rowdy, joviality.

Vesterbro and Frederiksberg

Conveniently placed, immediately west of Central Station, Vesterbro is where you may well find your accommodation for it is an area thick with hotels, and a couple of hostels. In less than an hour from grabbing luggage off the airport carousel you can be checking out your bedroom in Vesterbro. The area's main drag is Istedgade, running straight west from the back of the railway station, Europe's first official red-light area in the wake of 1970s Danish liberalization and now merging with a lively multi-cultural and semi-gentrified environment. Running parallel, one block to the north, the more seemly Vesterbrogade begins life at Rådhus-pladsen and runs west to bourgeois Frederiksberg and the green lawns of Frederiksberg Garden, a district that owes its air of easy living to a monarch's decision to build his summer residence here in the early 18th century.

Around the Three Lakes

The northern perimeter of Copenhagen is marked by three artificial lakes – Sortedams Sø, Peblinge Sø and Sankt Jørgens Sø – and the bridges that cross them connect an area rich in traditional cultural attractions with a bustling neighbourhood that reveals the sharp edge of contemporary Copenhagen. On the city side of the lakes lies the gratifying expanse of the Botanic Gardens and amid the surrounding parklands are to found the city's finest art galleries. All seems sedate and refined when juxtaposed with the working-class hustle and bustle of Nørrebro on the other side of the lakes. Historically a militant neighbourhood, this is where Denmark's trade unions struggled into existence a century ago. Nørrebro is again showing its mettle as its mixed population of first-generation immigrants and radical young Danes resist the country's turn to right-wing xenophobia.

Christiania and around

The 'free city' of bohemian Christiania and its infamous Pusher Street has been at odds with the Danish state for decades and is still subject to periodic police raids. It remains, deservedly, the main attraction on the island of Christianshavn, but it is not the only one. Lying to the east of Slotsholmen, Christianshavn was under water until reclaimed in the 17th century to provide fresh pastures for prospering city folk and Dutch merchants. A Dutch architect was commissioned to landscape the new town, pleasingly evident in the network of small canals that complement the higgledy-piggledy town houses with brightly-painted exteriors. The land reclamation also sought to provide the city with a military buttress, and exploring Christianshavn on foot opens up past history as much as Pusher Street in Christiania heralds a possible future.

★ **Ten of the best**

Best

1 **Room 606** A room in the Jacobsen-designed *Radisson SAS Royal Hotel*, completed in 1960, that has been retained exactly as it was first designed, p75.

2 **Nationalmuseet** Stupendous collection and some stunning displays of national historical treasures and pieces from Greenland and ancient Greece, p44.

3 **Illum Bolighus** Shopping for the finest Danish designer goods in one of the city's most prestigious stores, p199.

4 **Statens Museum for Kunst** Danish National Gallery, including non-Danish art, p80.

5 **Passagens Spisehus** Enjoy an evening of dishes from Greenland and Lapland – a tasty reminder of the city's Scandinavian heritage, p154.

6 **Børsen** Copenhagen's kooky stock exchange isn't open to the public but worth seeing from the outside anyway, p55.

7 **Christiania** Subversion from within, this area celebrates an alternative way of living (and relaxing), also with good restaurants, p90.

8 **Louisiana** World-class gallery of modern art with special exhibitions that in their own right would justify the easy trip out of town, p101.

9 **Frederiksborg Slot** Photogenic Renaissance castle, red-bricked and topped with copper spires. Worth the half hour trip out of town, p114.

10 **Viking Ship Museum** Excavated Viking ships sunk in Roskilde over 1,000 years ago. There is plenty to see and lots going on, especially in the summer, p114.

Trip planner

Copenhagen is a remarkably compact and small city. Many of the principal places of interest are within walking distance, and along the way you are likely to find yourself unashamedly shopping or browsing through the design shops. Excursions to major attractions like the Louisiana Gallery of Modern Art are easily organized and you could be standing in front of a Warhol in less than an hour after closing your hotel room.

May and June and the autumn period are ideal times, especially if getting a suntan or enjoying a summer festival atmosphere is not high on your list of priorities. The winter months are not forbiddingly cold, but temperatures commonly fall below zero between January and March, and the short daylight hours combined with a relentless grey sky will not enliven your spirits. Christmas is a twinkly affair but also a big family affair – consequently quite a lot of places close down on the day so as to celebrate in the home. In April the minimum temperature is about 3°C reaching the low 20°sC in June to August, and levelling out at around 10°C in September and October.

The price of a hotel room tends to increase in high season (July and August). Places are booked well in advance so make your reservations for rooms and restaurant tables in good time.

A day

The day could begin by looking around Rådhuspladsen and climbing the tower of the town hall for an aerial reconnaissance of the city. Shoppers might want to head straight for the pedestrianized shopping street Strøget, the parallel Vestergade and adjoining streets. Strøget terminates at Kongens Nytorv and on the other side of this illustrious square lie Nyhavn canal and a variety of cafés and restaurants, ideal for an indoor or al fresco *smørrebrød* lunch. Alternatively, an early breakfast would allow time to be outside the Nationalmuseet (National Museum) for opening time at 1000.

An afternoon could be spent exploring Slotsholmen, perhaps resting in the charming Bibliotekshaven before crossing the road to the Black Diamond and a drink in Øieblikket. Try to find time in the evening to visit Christiania, where there are also restaurants.

A weekend

The first day could be spent as above, with the next day starting by hopping on a bus or train to Nørrebro for a choice between clothes shopping or art galleries. The shopping is on the north side of the three lakes, especially along Blågårdsgade, the second street on your left off Nørrebrogade after crossing the bridge. A picnic in Assistens Kirkegård or lunch in one of the stylish pavement cafés in and around Sankt Hans Torv. An alternative morning's activity could be a visit to Denmark's national gallery, Statens Museum for Kunst, followed by a short walk to the Den Hirschsprungske Samling, a gallery of superb Danish art. Christiania could be explored in an afternoon. Before entering the 'free city', a visit to Vor Frelsers Kirke and a climb up the external staircase of the spiral tower would help reacquaint yourself with the geography of the city and its skyline. For dinner reserve a seat at the table in *Alberto K* at the *Radisson SAS Royal Hotel* and, on the strength of it, ask to be shown the original Jacobsen-designed room 606.

If the weekend is a long one, the modern art gallery of Louisiana is a major attraction, but so, too, is the small town of Helsingør. Another inland town competing for your time is Roskilde with its cathedral, a world heritage site, and the Viking Ship Museum.

A week

With a week to spend in Copenhagen there is no need to make a choice between the alternatives in the itineraries above. The Ny Carlsberg Glyptotek and the Royal Copenhagen Welcome Centre could also be visited. More time would allow for more excursions, a day sunbathing on the beaches, and a whole day in Malmö.

Contemporary Copenhagen

What makes contemporary Copenhagen tick? It depends on whom you ask. Cynics will say the city is canny and twee, smug even, while more sanguine commentators notice how Copenhageners sanely prioritize aspects of their lives, cutely saving money in order to attain what is ultimately worthwhile. Even on a short visit to the city, it is possible to observe these contrary claims to truth, and to realize that out of the apparent contradictions comes a healthy dynamic.

The city is remarkably civilized and well-behaved, and many non-American visitors are bemused by seeing pedestrians waiting patiently for a green light before crossing a road that was always devoid of traffic. This is not out of fear of a jaywalking charge – uniformed police are rarely seen – but more an expression of ingrained civic duty. If this makes Copenhageners sound too obedient, the Singaporeans of northern Europe, just take a bus to the 'free city' of Christiania where a community of some 800 citizens have enacted their right to run their own lives free of the State, and have been successfully doing so for over 30 years. And this doesn't mean that Christianites won't wait for the green light before crossing an empty road!

Copenhagen and its inhabitants have a delightful sense of modesty and proportion. Nude bathing is passé, but always in a designated area of a beach. What would surprise a city dweller is not the revelation that you're a bisexual with a penchant for s & m but an act of aggressive rudeness to a stranger. Aspects of the anarchist spirit of Christiania pervade everyday life as people go about their lives quietly, valuing their privacy in a way any bourgeois would approve, but also tolerating everyone's right to be different. And the sense of privacy is not English in character; witness the way many homes leave their curtains open at night as if indifferent to the public at large. The city's character is expressed in the urban skyline when viewed from the top of the town hall tower, where it is easy to read the landscape because there are so few high-rise buildings, only the very occasional tower block, a few church spires and a line of giant windmills out at sea. Nothing about Copenhagen is in your face.

On the buses that ply their way across the city it is easy to miss the two little flags of Denmark that flutter at the front of the vehicles. In their modest way they signify the subdued pride Copenhageners share in being Danish. It is not chauvinism, though there is often a note of imperial regret when Danes remind you that Greenland has home rule but is still part of the Danish Kingdom (forgetting to add that it's 95% ice, so who cares), as was Sweden, and national pride colours conversations about their near neighbours. This is normal for countries so close to one another, but in the last couple of years a nastier form of nationalism has shown itself in the election of far-right politicians, who as part of a coalition government, have introduced anti-immigrant regulations. There is a smugness that at its core says immigrants are welcome as long as they think and behave like Danes. Copenhageners like to socialize at home and keep work distinct from play – no pub lunches during workdays and pubbing after work is regarded with disdain. Not that you can accuse a city famous for its libertarian reforms in gender and sexual matters of puritanism. There is a touch of that glacial, Scandinavian worship of healthy living, but Copenhageners also smoke like troopers (looking for a non-smoking restaurant is a search for the Holy Grail) and decaf is regarded as an American aberration.

In the aesthetics of design and architecture, Copenhagen has every right to feel a cut above the European norm. This is not design à la Sunday colour supplements, the city is not on Planet Habitat, and at one extreme you can be forgiven for tipping ash into what is actually a designer side plate in a smart restaurant. It is with the vernacular that Danish design comes into its own, and window shopping in Illums Bolighus or Georg Jensen reveals just how sophisticated and tasteful Danish-designed cutlery, home furniture, silverware and glassware can be. Keep it simple and functional – to the point of stringency – is a guiding principle, from the sleek Viking ships of yesteryear to lego and the Christiania bicycle, and the latest shower fittings or Bang & Olufsen DVD player. You will experience it the moment you arrive at the new Terminal 3, designed by the celebrated Danish designer Vihelm Laurizen, and view its latest incarnation in the Øresund Bridge that connects Copenhagen with Sweden. See it at first hand when you visit the extension to Ny Carlsberg Glyptotek designed by Henning Larsen, or the museums of modern art at Louisiana and Arken. The roots of modern Danish design, functional but also experimental, are found in the achievements and influence of Arne Jacobsen, whose centenary was celebrated in 2002 and whose designs now grace many a smart restaurant in the city. Jacobsen's work was ahead of its time when he designed the lock, stock and barrel of the *Radisson SAS Royal Hotel* and much of what we take for granted today in terms of cool design was looked at askance when it first appeared some 50 years ago. Designs from the 1950s of Jacobsen's furniture and the famed lamps of Poul Henningsen are still exported, and the wooden chairs of Hans Wegner and the sofas of Erik Jørgensen are eagerly sought items.

And while svelte designs and flowing forms characterize the hip side of the city's character, lurking beneath is a yearning for herbal tea and healthy footwear, a deep need for cosiness and well-being summed up in a term – *hygee* – that has no adequate translation. The Copenhagen poet, Michael Strunge, called it bitterly "the life-support machine of this comatose state" but every now and again, encountering an error in a train timetable or someone's misguided street directions, the visitor is reminded that Danes are as human and fallible as the rest of us.

Travel essentials

Copenhagen can be reached by air, sea, coach, rail or car. Most visitors arrive by air, landing at Terminal 2 or 3 at Copenhagen International Airport and then taking the 12-minute train journey to Central Station (København H in Danish). A flight to Malmö in Sweden is also worth considering, and then using the fast bus or train routes over the bridge to Copenhagen. If you are outside of continental Europe, a flying is the best way. It won't save you time or money to go by road or rail.

Copenhagen's city centre is remarkably small and compact, and the best way to explore the sights is by walking or cycling. An integrated network of buses, local trains (S-Tog), and a new metro makes it easy to travel from one end of the city to the other. The tourist office (see p30) dispenses a free city map that details the main bus routes, train stations, hotels and sights. It may be wise to purchase a transport pass which will get you out to the furthest sights.

Getting there

Air

From UK and Europe There are frequent direct flights to Copenhagen with **Go** (now part of **easyJet**), **Scandinavian Airlines**, **Maersk Air**, **British Airways** and **BMI British Midland** from London, Birmingham, Manchester, Edinburgh and Dublin. **Go** is currently the cheapest carrier, flying from London Stansted (1 hour and 50 minutes) from £63 return, including taxes. **Ryanair** flies direct from London Stansted to Malmö, and from the airport there is a connecting bus service direct to Copenhagen, as well as trains departing every 20 minutes to Copenhagen from the station in Malmö and taking only 35 minutes. There are direct flights from all European capitals to Copenhagen International.

From US and Canada There are direct flights from east coast cities on **Scandinavian Airlines**, taking 7½ hours from New York, and 9½ hours from Seattle. Expect to pay around US$700 for a return ticket from the east coast.

Airport information Copenhagen International airport (**T** 32313231, flight information **T** 32474747, www.cph.dk) is 9 km from the city and 12 minutes from Central Station by a train service that runs every 20 minutes (Monday to Friday daily 0500-2400, Saturday 0530- 2400, Sunday 0630-2400) and costs 21kr. Some of these trains also stop at Nørreport, where a metro link with Kongens Nytorv accesses accommodation around Nyhavn. The train ticket office is in Terminal 3 (a shuttle bus connects Terminals 2 and 3), directly above the station, with a lift down to platform 1 for Copenhagen- bound trains. Buses and taxis depart from outside the airport and directions are clearly signposted. There is a city bus service, no 250S, that runs from the airport, costs about the same as the train but takes twice as long (40 minutes). Bus no 9 runs daily from the airport to Kongens Nytorv, handy for accommodation

Airlines and agents

Go, **T** 0870-6076543, www.go-fly.com
British Midlands, **T** 0870-6070555, www.flybmi.com
Maersk Air, **T** 207 3330066, www.maersk-air.com
Scandinavian Airlines, **T** 0845-60727727, www.scandinavian.net
British Airways, **T** 0845-7733377, www.britishairways.com
Ryan Air, **T** 0870-1569569, www.ryanair.com
Delta, **T** 1800-2414141, www.delta.com
North West Airlines, **T** 0870-5561000, www.nwa.com

Websites
www.trailfinders.com
www.sta-travel.com
www.travelcuts.com
www.travelocity.com
www.airbrokers.com

around Nyhavn, and there is a night bus, N96, that runs every half hour to an hour between the airport and city centre and costs 21kr (double on night bus). A taxi, from outside the arrivals hall, will cost about 150kr. Flybus 737 is a direct bus service between Copenhagen and Malmö airport (Sturup), with departure and arrival times scheduled to fit the Ryanair flights to and from London. From Copenhagen, it departs from Ingerslevsgade, opposite the DGI-byens Hotel, and from Malmö it departs from outside the airport. The one-way fare is 100kr and it can also be paid for in Swedish kr 120, €14 or £8.

Facilities include first-rate restaurants, a tourist office (0800-1900), money exchange (0630-2200), hotel booking desk (0600-2300), car hire, left luggage, banks and cash machines. Rooms can be booked for two to 16 hours at the airport's *Transfer Hotel* (**T** 32312455, email: transferhotel@cph.dk) for 240-990kr, and you don't need to have a room to use the hotel's sauna (95kr) and shower (80kr). There is also a Hilton Hotel at the airport (**T** 32501501, www.hilton.com).

Car
Travellers can bring a car on the **DFDS Seaways** Harwich-Esbjerg route and drive 200 km east to Copenhagen, or travel via the Channel Tunnel. The main European road routes to Copenhagen are the E47, E20 and E55. Journey time is two days and one night.

Coach
Eurolines run a bus service from London's Victoria Coach Station to Copenhagen's Central Station (www.gobycoach.com), costing from around £70 for a return apex fare. **Eurolines** also connects Copenhagen with many European cities, including Amsterdam, Frankfurt, Oslo, Paris and Stockholm. Again the journey takes two days and one night.

Ferry
DFDS Seaways run the Harwich-Esbjerg route, all year round, with departures every other day and taking 20 hours. There are ferries between Copenhagen and Malmö (35 minutes), Oslo (16 hours) and Swinoujscie in Poland (10 hours).

Train
Trains arrive at Copenhagen's Central Station from London's Liverpool Street using the **DFDS Seaways** Harwich-Esbjerg route, with connecting trains to Copenhagen (**T** 08705-333000). The price of a ticket is £342 in high season. There is also a **Eurostar** train service from London to Brussels with a connecting train to Copenhagen via Cologne and Hamburg (**Rail Europe**, **T** 0870-5848848). A return fare costs around £250. There are rail links between Copenhagen and all European capitals, and regular daily trains between Copenhagen and Malmö in Sweden. Central Station

has fast-food outlets and restaurants, post office, money exchange, bicycle rental, a left-luggage office, and a supermarket that closes at midnight.

Getting around

Public transport tickets cover buses, S-Tog trains and the metro within designated zonal areas. The basic ticket costs 14kr and covers travel within any two zones – which in central Copenhagen covers all the sights and places of interest – and allows for transfers between buses, trains and metro for up to one hour. Tickets and maps showing the zones are available from machines or ticket offices in train stations and from bus drivers.

Discount clip cards (*klippekort*) covering 10 journeys, available in stations but not from bus drivers, work out cheaper than individual tickets. You punch the card in a yellow card-clipping machine on a bus, station or local train. A two-zone card costs 80kr and by clipping the card more than once you can travel in more zones than the card allows. A 24-hour ticket, purchased at bus and train stations, gives unlimited travel by bus and train through all the zones and costs 85kr. It has to be clipped in the yellow machines at the first station or bus you use.

Bus

The city's bus routes, comprehensive and efficient, are marked on the free map dispensed by the tourist office and available in most hotels. The central bus station and information centre is at Rådhuspladsen and you may also find yourself using the bus stops outside the Tivoli side of Central Station and the Vesterport side. Useful routes include the No 5 from Rådhuspladsen to Nørreport, Nørrebrogade and Assistens Kirkegård; No 6 from Central Station to Vesterbro, Frederiksborg Slot and the Zoo in one direction and Slotsholmen, Nyhavn and Experimentarium in the other; No 8 from Central Station or Rådhuspladsen to Christiania; No 16 from

Copenhagen Card

The Copenhagen Card, www.copenhagencard.dk, is a travel pass issued by the tourist office and available through many hotels, offering unlimited travel on buses, trains and metro in the Greater Copenhagen area (which includes towns like Helsingør, Hillerød, Roskilde) and free admission to most museums and sights. Valid for between 24, 48 and 72 hours, costing 215kr, 375kr, 495kr (children's tickets available), the Card would only pay for itself if you intend to visit a lot of museums and take more than one excursion out of town.

Rådhuspladsen to Carlsberg Brewery and to Nørrebrogade and Assistens Kirkegård. Night buses, bearing 'N' before the bus number, ply a few routes and fares are doubled. Buses bearing an 'S', like the 250S from the airport, are fast buses that do not stop at every bus stop. See Directory, p229, for contact details.

A harbour bus service connects the Black Diamond building with stops along the waterfront, including Nyhavn and Holmen North. Buses travel throughout the day, 0600-1825, six times per hour, and cost 28kr or can be used with the clip card.

Car

There is little or no point in the visitor having a car to use in and around Copenhagen. The city centre is a tiny area, many streets are pedestrianized, and parking and petrol are expensive. Even for excursions, public transport is more than adequate. Car hire companies have desks at the airport, but the best deals are arranged before you arrive. If you do need to drive, the *Copenhagen This Week* booklet, available from the tourist office, has detailed information on speed limits and parking options around the city. See Directory, p224, for details of car hire.

Cycling

Without actually banning the automobile, Copenhagen is as cycle-friendly as you can get, and hiring a bike for part or all of your trip is well worth considering. Cycle lanes are everywhere and cyclists overtake on the left of the lane, so generally keep to the right and remember that bus passengers always have the right of way at bus stops so wait for the bus doors to shut before continuing. To indicate to other cyclists that you are about to stop cycling, raise your right hand. Between April and September, there is a citywide system of public bike rentals that operates like supermarket trolleys (www.bycyklen.dk). A 20kr coin is inserted in a slot to free a bike from one of the bike deposit areas, usually outside an S-Tog station, and reclaimed when the bike is returned. It's easy to recognize the bikes through their solid wheels and the conspicuous advertisement of the sponsor. It sounds a great idea, but the gearless bikes take a hammering over the course of each summer and are only good for the occasional short journey or two; much better to hire a decent bike. All bikes can be taken on STog-trains for 12kr (a bicycle *klippekort* is available), though not during rush hours (Monday to Friday 0700-0830 travelling into the city and 1530-1700 travelling out). Look for a carriage with a cycle symbol on the door. See Directory, p224, for details of bicycle hire.

Metro

Copenhagen's new metro system of underground trains came on line in early 2003 with a line connecting Christianshavn with Nørreport via Kongens Nytorv.

Taxi

Taxis ready for hire carry a sign with the word FRI (free) on display, and there is a taxi rank outside Central Station. The basic fare is

! If you look for the driver of a metro train you won't find one – the trains are fully automatic.

Robotic rails

At Kongens Nytorv Copenhageners enjoy their new underground system – fully automated, it is state-of-the-art.

22kr, then 10kr per km, or 11kr on Sunday and between 1500 and 0600, or 13kr between 1100 and 0600 on Friday and Saturday. Most accept payment by credit card. There are also bike taxis for two passengers which can be hailed in the street and found around key sights and the railway station; cost between 25kr and 90kr. See Directory, p228, for contact details of firms.

Train
The S-Tog train service is easy to navigate and with nearly all the routes passing through Central Station it is hard to get lost. Running from around 0500 to 1430, one variable is the speed of the train, and with fast trains not stopping at every station check the information panel on the platform or ask a fellow traveller. **Danish State Railways** (DSB) operates local trains that connect Copenhagen with Helsingør (every 20 mins) and Roskilde, stopping at Østerport and Nørreport stations and some local suburban stations. Trains run to Malmö every 20 minutes from Central Station between 0520 and 0040, with night trains at 0120, 0220, 0320 and 0420, taking 35 minutes. See Directory, p229, for contact details and the inside back cover for the map.

Walking
It is easy and very safe to get around the various sights on foot. From Central Station it takes about half an hour to walk the length of Ströget and reach Nyhavn on foot. From accommodation around Istedgade or Vesterbrogade, the main hotel area, it takes 20 minutes to reach Slotsholmen. The city centre area is small and self-contained, with a number of pedestrianized streets and squares, and walking tours are an option, see p30.

Tours

Bus tours

Open Top Tours, **T** 32540606, www.cex.dl, run an open-bus
tour with a commentary of all the main sights, running from just
before Easter to the end of October and costing 100-125kr
depending on the length of time (45, 60, 75 minutes). Departure
point is Rådhuspladsen (Town Hall Square), which is where its
longer tours to Sweden (June to mid-September, Monday and
Friday, 415kr), Malmö (mid-May to June and August to mid-
September, Tuesday and Thursday, 345kr); Roskilde (May to
August, 360kr), Hillerød (May, Tuesday; June to August Tuesday,
Thursday, Saturday and Sunday; September, Tuesday and
Thursday and October Saturday, 330kr), Copenhagen (1100
daily and May-September 1330, and October to May 1430 on
Saturday). There is also the Hop On-Hop Off bus (**T** 38280188,
www.citysightseeing.dk) that departs from Rådhuspladsen, with
stops throughout the city. The cost is 80kr; the night bus tour is
100kr. The same company run out-of-town tours along the lines
of Open Top Tours above.

   Copenhagen Excursions, **T** 32540606, starts its tours from
Rådhuspladsen and tickets can be booked through hotels or just
turn up and purchase from the tour guide.

Canal tours

Between late March and late October, **DFDS Canal Tours**
conducts 50-minute, 50-kr guided tours through the harbour and
canals, departing at 1000 and then every half hour until 1700 from
the city end of Nyhavn Canal or from Gammel Strand. Between
21 June and 25 August, tours depart from Nyhavn until 1930.

Walking tours
Copenhagen Walking Tours depart from the Wonderful Copenhagen tourist office, Monday to Saturday at 1030, to various parts of the old city, lasting two hours, 75kr. A separate Walking Tour of Old City of Copenhagen departs every Saturday and Sunday from the same location at 1100 for the same price. Guided walks based around different themes can be booked in advance at the tourist office, **T** 33464646, www.meetthedanes.dk. Guided walks around Christiania depart at 1500 from inside the 'free city' on Saturday and Sunday at 1500 throughout the year for 30kr, **T** 32579670.

Tourist information

The **Wonderful Copenhagen** tourist office, **T** 70222442, is on the corner of Vesterbrogade and Bernstorffsgade, close to Central Station, open between May and August, Monday to Saturday, from 0900-2000 and on Sunday from 1000-1800. The rest of the year it's open Monday-Friday 0900 to 1630 and to 1330 on Saturday. You can collect a free map of the city, a copy of *Copenhagen This Week* (published fortnightly), seek information on transport, sights and events, purchase the Copenhagen Card, book sightseeing tours and accommodation. There is a smaller tourist office at the airport.

Copenhagen Post, www.cphpost.dk, is a weekly newspaper in English that appears on Friday, 15kr, sold at the tourist office, various hotels and restaurants. As well as Danish news, there is a useful day-by-day schedule of entertainment events.

Rådhuspladsen and around, 33 Historic city square, twinkly Tivoli, shopping mecca rubbing shoulders with university Latin quarter.

Slotsholmen and around, 43 Chic pavement restaurants gazing across canal waters to an island stuffed with museums, a castle, a myriad of architectural delights.

Nyhavn and around, 58 Not exactly je ne sais quoi but something special here, a Scandinavian buzz around the pavement cafés celebrating the good life.

Vesterbro and Frederiksberg, 72 Chalk and cheese: a semi-proletarian quarter, sex shops galore, running into a salubrious neighbourhood spiked into life by summer jazz festivities.

Around the Three Lakes, 79 Landscaped lakes and botanic gardens provide muted background to street-wise, rebellious Nørrebro.

Christiania and around, 90 The twee and sober side of Denmark riotously subverted by Nordic chutzpa, not to be missed.

Rådhuspladsen and around

Before mid-morning you can have the wide open space of Rådhuspladsen almost to yourself, with only the gentle buzz of commuters flowing around you on foot, bike or car, and the late 19th and early 20th-century buildings looking down on you. This is an ideal time to explore the city's main public square before nearby **Ny Carlsberg Glyptotek**, *a major cultural attraction, opens its door. The most hyped street in Copenhagen,* **Strøget**, *begins to hum with consumers from late morning onwards and by lunchtime its open-air cafés, restaurants and cobbled squares are heaving with people and street performers. Discerning travellers ignore the crowds and head off to explore the more interesting shops that are tucked away down the narrow side streets. This is where the Copenhagen of medieval times developed, but for a more tangible feel of the past move on a few centuries and delve about in the streets around the university and some grand 19th-century churches. The* **university building** *on Frue Plads is worth a look and, even though most academic departments have moved out from here, there is a studious feel to this part of town and the atmosphere is pleasantly calm. For more bustle, head back to Rådhuspladsen in the evening and the twinkly lights of* **Tivoli**.

▶▶ *See Sleeping p123, Eating and drinking p141 and Shopping p193*

◉ Sights

★ Ny Carlsberg Glyptotek (Carlsberg Sculpture Centre)
Dantes Plads 7, T33418141, www.glyptoteket.dk   *Tue-Sun 1000-1600. Adults 30kr, children free. Sun and Wed free.   Buses 1, 10, 28, 550S, 650S, and those stopping at Rådhuspladsen.   Map 3, E5, p252*

Architecturally grand both inside and out, especially with the 1996 gallery designed by Henning Larsen, Ny Carlsberg Glyptotek is one of

★ **Best**

Museums

the city's must-see places of culture. Founded by Carl Jacobsen and named after his brewery, Glyptotek (sculpture collection) was added a little misleadingly given that the beer magnate (p75) was an equally avid collector of French and Danish art. Like other world-class museums, there is too much to take in on a single visit and a return trip is worth considering. On a first visit it may be worth opting for either the extensive ancient Near East and Mediterranean collections or the 19th-century French paintings; or make a judicious choice from the many rooms of ancient art before heading for the modern collections. Also bear in mind that the small but superb collection of Archaic and Classical Greek pottery is located downstairs as part of the Etruscan collection, in room 20, because they happened to be found in Italy. To make a beeline for the renowned French art, after entering the Winter Garden do not go up the steps on the far side but turn to the left just before them and pass through the glass doors. This leads to the sparkling new wing of the museum and the Impressionists are in rooms 61/2 – Monet, Renoir, Pissarro, Degas and Cézanne – and to Gauguin and his Tahitian girls, van Gogh and Toulouse-Lautrec in rooms 63-6. (Gauguin lived in Copenhagen for a time.) You are not likely to forget the magnificent glass-domed and tiled Winter Garden conservatory. There are benches amidst the giant palm trees, Roman sarcophagi and contemporary Danish sculptures. The café is also a treat (p144).

The 2kr ground plan is worth having, but the really useful subject catalogues in the bookshop are pricey at around 160kr each. Laminated cards highlighting exhibits are freely available in only some of the rooms, but quite a lot of the exhibits are poorly labelled and inadequately described.

Tivoli

Vesterbrogade 3, **T** 33151001, www.tivoligardens.com *19 Apr-22 Sep Mon-Thu, Sun 1100-2400, Fri-Sat 1100-0100, 15 Dec-23 Dec Mon-Wed, Sun 1100-2100, Thu-Sat 1100-2200. Adults 55kr, children 30. Buses 1, 2, 6, 8, 10-16, 28-30, 34, 40, 67-69, 150S, 550S, 650S. Map 3, D4, p252*

The Tivoli amusement park, the most visited attraction in Denmark let alone Copenhagen, first opened its pleasure gardens in 1843, and when it was put up for sale in 1999 the hullabaloo that followed ensured it was kept in Danish hands. Tivoli is a national institution (most visitors are Danes) and a visit seems almost obligatory but, unless young children are in tow, it is hugely overrated and best enjoyed as a shrine to cuteness, especially on Saturday and Sunday evenings at 1730 and 1930 when a parade of mock-toy soldiers – the **Tivoli Boys Guard** – and gilded carriages wind their way through the crowds. The tweeness of Tivoli encourages Disneyfication, helped by the likes of Sting, Phil Collins and the Beach Boys appearing on stage, but a glimmer of the original Orient-inspired magic still pervades the place when twilight descends and neon-less, muted lighting illuminates the Turkish facade of *Restaurant Nimb* outside the silent fountain inspired by the concepts of Niels Bohr, the Danish winner of the Nobel Prize for physics. The Chinese-style **Pantomime Theatre** plays host to a genuine ghost of *commedia dell'arte*, there is an

! During the Second World War, Poul Henningsen circumvented Nazi-imposed black out regulations by inventing horizontal light lamps so that the light could not be seen from above, allowing Tivoli to remain open after sunset.

ancient rollercoaster and smaller echoes of times past that are worth seeking out, like the 1949 spiral lamp of the designer Poul Henningsen near Tivoli Lake. Henningsen contributed much to the rebuilding of Tivoli after the Second World War and his stunning **Glassalen** (The Glass Hall), with its hint of camp, should not be missed (from the entrance opposite Central Station, keep straight ahead, crossing the seating area of the open-air stage). **Tivoli Lake**, especially attractive when the flower borders are in full bloom and the light-filled dragonflies are switched on, is another piece of history; surviving from the 1840s when the park lay outside the city's boundaries and made use of the original moat that once fortified Copenhagen.

There are nearly 40 places serving food, ice cream and sweet pastries in Tivoli, more or less all overpriced, ranging from fast food outlets to superior fish restaurants like *La Crevette* (see p141). In summer time, at 2345 on Wednesday and Saturday nights, there is a firework display.

Rådhuset and around

Rådhuspladsen, **T** *33662582, www.copenhagencity.dk Mon-Fri 0800-1700, Sat 0930-1300. Free. Guided tours Mon-Fri 1500, Sat 1000 and 1100. Adults 30kr. City Hall Tower Jun-Sep Mon-Fri 1000, 1200, 1400, Sat 1200. Oct-May Mon-Sat 1200. Adults 20kr. Jens Olsen's World Clock Mon-Fri 1000-1600, Sat 1000-1300. Adults 10kr, children 5kr. Buses 2, 6, 8, 11, 14, 16, 28, 29, 30, 34, 67, 68, 69, 173E, 150S, 250S. Map 3, D5, p252*

Copenhagen's **Town Hall**, built between 1892 and 1905 and a de facto landmark building given its function and location, benefits from a flourish of architectural styles from the graceful to the whimsical. The predominately brown-brick exterior seems prosaic from a distance, but gazing up from outside the nondescript entrance, topped by a small balcony and a gilded statue of Bishop Absalon, brings into play a line of six carved figures standing alert. Smaller carvings are dotted about the exterior walls and as the eye takes them in a surreptitious playfulness becomes apparent in the design. This becomes more obvious once inside the building and you are free to wander about and spot the capricious decorative details on the brickwork and stonework, like the carved doves and beetles nonchalantly carved into a pillar on the first floor. Murals, mosaic floors and painted ceilings complete the visual feast.

The climb up the 105.6-m tower affords fine views but a visit to the highly complex **Jens Olsen's World Clock** is definitely not for the horologically-challenged.

The statues around Rådhuset are worth checking out: Hans Christian Andersen is here of course, but more striking is the statue in front of it enacting an encounter between a mammal and a monster, in the centre of a fountain fed by the mouths of sinister sea creatures. On the other side of the square stands a pillar topped with a stone statue of two manly Vikings blowing those S-shaped horns called lurs (p114). Facing this statue, on Vester Voldgade, is the refined-looking Palace Hotel, contemporaneous with Rådhuset and built to accommodate visiting burghers, but with a disappointing interior as a result of an unimaginative renovation. Next door, deflating the luxury hotel's pretensions, is the anodyne **Ripley's Believe It Or Not! Museum** (p221). What is worth noting is back across the square where, literally on the corner of Vesterbrogade on the building with the Philips flag, the day's temperature is recorded with the aid of a golden girl, a bicycle and an umbrella. Also here, on HC Andersens Boulevard, is the **Louis Tussaud's Wax Museum**, as interesting for its 1897 building as for the wax effigies standing about inside.

! Jens Olsen's World Clock took nearly 30 years to construct. All the gears and cogs are on show, plus the solar systems and lines of orbit. You can just about make out what time it is!

Riding high
Bishop Absalon's Statue casts a shadow against the stately buildings of Højbro Plads.

Dansk Design Centre (Danish Design Centre)

HC Andersens Boulevard 27, **T** 33693369, www.ddc.dk *Mon-Fri 1000-1700, Sat-Sun 1130-1600. Adults 30kr, children 15kr. Buses 1, 2, 5, 6, 8, 10, 28-30, 32, 33, 550S, 650S. Map 3, D5, p252*

The value of a visit here depends a lot on the quality of the temporary exhibitions being mounted. In 2002 there was a celebrated exhibition marking the centenary of Arne Jacobsen's birth, plus the work of Japanese paper designers, and there should always be two or three new shows taking place. Downstairs, there is a permanent display of winners of the Industrial Design Prize between 1965-99 (now replaced by the Danish Design Prize), featuring Lego, early typewriters, cash registers, vacuum cleaners, industrial suits, telephones, the LP cover of the Sgt Pepper's Lonely Hearts Club Band album and lots more. There is a great shop and a café (see p144) that serves pleasant lunches. Henning Larsen designed the centre but not all of his ideas for the building were brought to fruition, as information panels near the entrance explain.

Lower Strøget
Map 3, grid C5/B6, p252 See also p193

Strøget (pronounced 'stroll'), referred to as 'the walking street', is the collective name for a series of linked pedestrianized streets – Frederiksbergade, Nygade, Vimmelskafet, Amagertorv and Østergade – and much hyped as a grand shopping experience. Don't believe it, for with a few noted exceptions like **Illums Bolighus**, **Holmegaard**, **Georg Jensen**, and **Royal Copenhagen** on Amagertorv, and a couple on Østergade at the upper end of Strøget, this street's shopping is mostly spoilt by irksome international brand names. What does make all of Strøget tick, though, is the human traffic – especially around the adjoining squares of **Gammeltorv** and **Nytorv** ('old square' and 'new square') that Strøget bisects just a couple of blocks up from

I am choking on aesthetics

Arne Jacobsen

Grand designs

"I painted my room white, my parents thought it was barbaric – over the expensive wallpaper with the colourful patterns."

Still probably the greatest Danish designer, the centenary of Arne Jacobsen's death was celebrated to much acclaim in 2002 with special exhibitions at Louisiana, the Danish Design Centre and the Museum of Modern Art in Oxford (he designed St Catherine's College). Trained as an architect and with over 350 works to his name, from a hotel (see p75) and bank (see p55) to doorhandles and ashtrays, Jacobsen modified the Scandinavian fetish for the linear and functional with sinuous, organic shapes and his designs are still exported throughout the world. His famous chairs, as well as seating Bond villains, attained an iconic status with that 1960s photograph of a naked Christine Keeler sitting legs akimbo on one. His stackable Ant chair, with the seat and back formed and pressed in one piece, was designed for the cafeteria of a medical company. Jacobsen continues to define the luminous characteristics of Danish design – quality materials, an aesthetic functionalism and what critics dubbed the "visual expression of a socially just society". www.arne-jacobsen.com

Rådhuspladsen. Gammeltorv is distinguished by the **Caritas Fountain**, a highly attractive piece of Renaissance art (1608), rebuilt at the end of the nineteenth century, depicting Charity as a woman with water from her breasts sprinkling over two children. The contrasting attraction in Nytorv is the severe-looking **Domhuset** (Courthouse) fronted by neoclassical columns that suggest anything but charity. The building was the city's town hall as well as courthouse, until 1905 when Rådhuset was completed, opening in 1815 on the site of the first town hall that had divided the two squares. The building in Nytorv that is now a bank occupies the ground of a house where Kierkegaard once lived, while Gammeltorv covers the ground of Copenhagen's medieval marketplace.

● *Don't get fooled. Good shopping is not the same as good advertising, so forget Lower Strøget and explore instead parallel Vestergade and the smaller streets running off it.*

Slotsholmen and around

For its small square acreage, no other part of Copenhagen can compare with the island of Slotsholmen and its immediate vicinity in terms of buildings worth seeing, museums worth exploring and parks worth relaxing in. Immediately to the west of the island stands the **Nationalmuseet** *(National Museum) with its incomparable collection of historical and cultural artefacts, while on Slotsholmen itself there is a mystifying complex of historical buildings that will take time to sort out and identify and most of a day to explore. Opening hours are confusingly different and a visit on a Sunday, after mid-morning, is the ideal time to catch most places open. If pressed for time, try at least to fit in time to see the ruins of the original* **12th-century castle** *in* **Christiansborg Slot** *(Palace), which are more interesting than the Royal Reception Rooms or the Danish Parliament that are part of the same palace structure. Also worth viewing is the collection of sculptures in the* **Thorvaldsen***, though anyone with an interest in architecture will check out the* **Black Diamond***, the very curious stock exchange building (Børsen) and the neighbouring bank designed by Arne Jacobsen. The placid* **Kongens Have** *(Royal Garden) makes an ideal picnic spot and there is always* **Gammel Strand** *facing the northern canal with its open-air cafés and restaurants.*

▸▸ *See Sleeping p125 and Eating and drinking p145*

◉ Sights

★ Nationalmuseet (National Museum)

Ny Vestergade 10, **T** 33693369, www.natmus.dk *Tue-Sun 1000-1700. Adults 40kr, children free, Wed free. Buses 1, 2, 5, 6, 8, 10, 28-30, 32, 33, 550S, 650S. Map 3, D6, p252*

Denmark's National Museum lays claim to four floors of world cultural history with more than a modicum of justification. The emphasis is naturally on Denmark but there is an expansive ethnographical collection as well as a floor devoted to Near East and Classical antiquities. Like Ny Carlsberg Glyptotek, trying to see everything could prove exhausting and counter-productive but the free day encourages a return visit.

The entrance leads into a large chamber, all lightness of being, with the rooms of Danish prehistory on the right, and a balcony café at the far end of the hall above the shop. The ground floor rooms devoted to early Denmark, from the reindeer-hunting Ice Age to the Vikings, have some astounding artefacts deposited as offerings in bogs some three millennia ago: weapons, shields, swords, sacred drinking vessels, lurs (Bronze Age sacred musical instruments), and horned helmets straight out of a Hollywood version of Viking times. The proper Viking age, AD750-1050, accounts for the treasure hoards of silver ornaments, jewellery, coins and skin cloaks in rooms 20-22, including an awesome display of finds from a bog where battle victors heaped up their enemies' dead horses and weapons. After hacking the weapons to pieces they were offered to the gods, presumably as a sacrifice of thanksgiving. In room 13 there is a spectacular chariot from first-century BC Jutland and in room 11 an oak coffin, Bronze Age graves of fully-clothed men buried with their swords and personal belongings (comb, razor and spare cap). Room 11 also leads to a room with an exquisite cult chariot driven by horses carrying a miniature sun across the sky. Room 6 has another astonishing display, a single sacrificial gift of over 4,000 amber beads placed in a bog in northern Jutland.

The first and second floors' ethnographic collections comprise a dizzying quantity of artefacts from around the world, the most unique belonging to the Inuits and including an Eskimo hunter's anorak made of depilated, waterproof sealskin that beats anything seen in a specialist sports shop. The third floor has some fine Classical-Age antiquities, including a metope from the outer frieze of the Parthenon that was purchased by a Danish naval officer in the 17th century. The black- and red-figure pottery from fifth-century Greece includes some fine work, especially in rooms 306 and 310. Look for the cup of a symposium scene by the Brygos painter, showing a man on a couch vomiting while his servant holds his forehead, and the vase showing Athena escorting Heracles to Olympia in a chariot, accompanied by Apollo, Artemis and wing-footed Hermes.

Christiansborg Slot

Christiansborg Slotsplads, *T* 33926492, www.ses.dk *Ruins under the palace May-Sep, 0930-1530. Jan-Apr and Oct-Dec, Tue, Thu, Sat, Sun 0930-1530. Adults 20kr, children 5kr. Royal Reception Rooms, May- Sep, guided tours 1300, 1500. Jan-Apr, guided tours, Tue, Thu, Sat, Sun, 1100, 1500. Adults 40kr, children 10kr. Buses 1, 2, 6, 8, 9, 10, 19, 28, 29, 31, 32, 37, 550S, 650S. Map 3, C7, p253*

The ruins of Bishop Absalon's stone fort built in 1167 were only discovered at the start of the 20th century when the foundations were being excavated for the present-day palace. It may take some discovery work on your part to find the entrance, a door to the right of the main archway as you stand facing the palace with the equestrian statue in Christiansborg Slotsplads behind you. The present underground exhibition is very well presented, with all the information available in English, and manages to bring archaeology

Christianborg Slot
A complex of parts of palaces, castles and royal buildings, it is worth a visit just to see the Danish Parliament in session – a very informal affair.

▶ Sorting out Christiansborg

Sorting out what is where and when it was built in Christiansborg – a complex of parts of palaces, castles and sundry royal buildings – can be a headache because everything seems to be hidden behind a nondescript door, with small signs that you tend to only notice on the way out. The austere grey building with the green copper spire is Christiansborg Palace (Slot), best entered from its east side which fronts Christiansborg Slotsplads (Palace Square) and its statue of Frederik VII in a classic equestrian pose.

alive. In a display room to the side of the excavated walls and wells, there are interesting finds from the archaeological dig of 1907, like axle marks clearly visible in some of the limestone blocks, and informative histories of the palaces telling, for example, that beech trees were felled in their thousands to provide pilings for modernization work in the 1720s.

To find the way to the **Royal Reception Rooms**, walk through the archway from Christiansborg Slotsplads and look for the entrance door on your right. The rooms, still used by Danish royalty for official receptions, are described in the guided tours and worth noting are the modern wall tapestries and the frieze by Thorvaldsen, the Danish sculptor. If you like this example of his work, be sure to visit Thorvaldsen's Museum (see below).

Folketinget (Danish Parliament)

Christiansborg Slot, Christiansborg Slotsplads, T 33375500, www.folketing.dk *Free to public gallery during parliamentary sessions. Free guided tours, 3 Jul-24 Sep, 1400, and on Sun throughout the year at 1400. Buses 1, 2, 6, 8, 9, 10, 19, 28, 29, 31, 32, 37, 550S, 650S. Map 3, C7, p249*

Standing back outside the main archway in Christiansborg Slotsplads with the equestrian statue behind you, turn left and walk around the building to find Folketinget on your right side. A visit during a parliamentary session offers a tremendous contrast with the formalities of the British House of Commons, but to learn more it is worth joining one of the English-language tours. The political geography of the seating arrangements is explained and there is an opportunity to find out who's who in the collection of political paintings on display.

Kongelige Stalde Og Kareter (Royal Stables and Coaches)
Christiansborg Ridebane, **T** 33401010, www.kongehuset.dk
May-Sep, Fri-Sun 1400-1600. Oct-Apr, Sat-Sun 1400-1600. Adults 20kr, children 10kr. Map 3, C7, p249

The moderately interesting **Royal Transport Museum**, composed of a car, coaches and accoutrements, is less engaging than the stables themselves, which are extravagantly flamboyant in style and must have made the 200 resident horses feel mighty privileged.

    Teatermuseet (Theatre Museum), *Sun 1200-1800, Wed 1400-1600, Sat 1200-1600, adults 30kr, children 5kr,* is above the Royal Stables and Coaches and occupies the site of an 18th-century court theatre inaugurated by Frederick V. It remained in use until 1881 and opened as a theatre museum some 40 years later. The theatrical exhibits are none too enticing but the actual auditorium is a grand affair, adorned with a luxuriously painted ceiling.

    Tøjhusmuseet (Royal Arsenal Museum), *Tue-Sun 1200-1600, adults 40kr, children free,* is to the south of the Royal Stables and Coaches on the other side of the road. The long vaulted room is the longest of its kind at 163 m and it needs to be to house the staggeringly large collection of guns, cannon, artillery and tanks on display. You think you've seen the lot, and then upstairs there is another vast accumulation of assorted weapons that will leave

★ **Traditional Danish Architecture**

you exhausted just contemplating the collection. Anyone with an interest in arms and armour should consider planning their visit in isolation from the other museums in Slotsholmen and give the Royal Arsenal the undivided attention it demands.

If entering Slotsholmen from the west side, from the National Museum along Ny Vestergade and across a small bridge, don't mistake this square with the large courtyard that you find yourself in. Here there is also an equestrian statue (Christian IX), with stables and carriage buildings either side, and you need to walk straight across the courtyard and out the other side to reach Christiansborg Palace Square.

The Christiansborg Slot you see today was built at the start of the 20th century to house the royal family and the parliament. It replaced an earlier palace that was completed in the 1820s only to burn to the ground some 60 years later. The palace of the 1820s was itself a replacement for an earlier palace built in the 1730s under the direction of king Christian VI and it was from his name that the title of Christiansborg came. All three of these palaces occupy the site of the original stone fort built by Bishop Absalon in the 12th century, and this original castle was itself replaced with a new castle that was built in the early 15th century. Various additions were made to this second castle over the following two centuries until the newly crowned Christian VI came along and chose to make a name for himself by not just throwing out the chintz but demolishing the entire castle and building a new palace. So the copper-spired Christiansborg Slot that graces contemporary Copenhagen is the fifth grand building on the same site.

Thorvaldsen's Museum

Porthusgade 2, **T** 33321532, www.thorvaldsenmuseum.dk
Tue-Sun 1000-1500. Adults 20kr, children free, Wed free. Buses 1, 2, 6, 8, 9, 10, 19, 28, 29, 31, 32, 37, 550S, 650S. Map 3, C7, p253

Wander through this museum at leisure and the chances are you will encounter a figure of someone or other you admire because the sculptor Bertel Thorvaldsen was a workaholic capable of putting a factory production line to shame. Born in 1768, he lived in Rome for 40 years before returning to his home city of Copenhagen to spearhead a cultural and artistic nationalism. His long sojourn in Italy helps account for the preponderance of classical subjects; Jason and Venus crop up more often than you might want and Ganymedes are everywhere. A catalogue would need to be purchased to identify the subject matter of the many small friezes, and there are countless busts on pillars of forgotten celebrities of their day. The huge Hercules on the stairs, very well-executed but with a hint of that blandness that characterizes Roman copies of Greek originals, suggests a drawback to Thorvaldsen's prodigious output, but there is no denying the power of his monumental style, and his portraits of the Twelve Apostles and Christ have an iconic status that can still impress. Outside the museum, a new reflective geometric pool invites speculation. Designed to suggest 'movement with movement with movement', judge for yourself whether it succeeds.

● *Take a coffee break in the hall off the reception/shop area of Thorvaldsen's Museum and relax – if you can – under a truly colossal statue of Maximilian I with a giant Gutenberg alongside him.*

Christiansborgs Slotskirke (Palace Chapel)

Christiansborg Slotsplads, **T** 33926451. *Jul 1200-1600. Jan-Jun and Aug-Dec, Sun 1200-1600. Free. Buses 1, 2, 6, 8, 9, 10, 19, 28, 29, 31, 32, 37, 550S, 650S. Map 3, C7, p253*

Next door to Thorvaldsen's Museum, the worshipper-free Christiansborgs Slotskirke was built in the neoclassical style in the 1820s and managed to survive the 1884 fire that destroyed the second Christiansborg Slot only to succumb to another fire in 1992 that brought the roof down when a firework from festivities landed on it. Meticulously restored to its pristine state, the glossy interior makes it clear that the architect, HC Hansen, had little interest in matters spiritual but really knew how to imitate classical models and motifs. If nothing else, a visit here affords a splendid opportunity to appreciate the Corinthian style of Greek column at close quarters.

● *Exploring Slotsholmen can prove exhausting and there are two escape routes: northwards across the canal to Gammel Strand and its restaurants (see p145), or southwards to the Bibliotekshaven (Royal Library Garden) for a rest and possible picnic.*

Gammel Strand

Map 3, C6/7, p252/253

Gammel Strand, free of traffic and offering the best view of Slotsholmen, was the commercial heart of Copenhagen in medieval times. Fresh fish were landed here and sold by the fishermen's wives, hence the statue of one of them near the bridge that connects Slotsholmen with Højbro Plads (see p62). Another link with Gammel Strand's past is evident in the cafés and restaurants specializing in fish dishes (see p145) but modernity makes a welcome intrusion in the form of **Kunstforegningen** at No 48, Tue-Sun 1100-1700, 30kr. It is an important exhibition space for art and photography and nearly always worth a visit.

★ **Views**

Best

- Slotsholmen from cobbled Gammel Strand, p52
- View of the city from the tower of Rådhuset, p36
- Looking across to Sweden from Marmorkirken's dome, p65
- Gazing down on the city from a window table at the *Alberto K*, p153
- Cityscape from Vor Frelsers Kirke, p92

● *If you are tired of walking the DFDS Canal Tours (see p29) depart from Gammel Strand.*

Bibliotekshaven (Royal Library Garden)

Rigdagsgården. *0600-2200. Free.* Buses 1, 2, 6, 8, 10, 37, 550S, 650S. Map 3, D8, p253

Bibliotekshaven, secreted behind an ivy-clad wall that was once the entrance to the old royal library, is a haven of quietness, especially at weekends when at times you may have the grounds to yourself. It's hard to believe you are standing in what was once a dockyard, but a mooring ring for ships has been built into the north wall as a reminder of the past. The park has a pond with a little duck house, and a water sculpture that spouts water every hour on the hour, and looking out across it – to where his fiancée Regine Olsen is said to have lived – stands a statue of a melancholy Søren Kierkegaard with a quill in his hand. Benches are spaced out around the margins of the park, the perfect spot for a rest and a chapter or two of *Miss Smilla's Feeling for Snow* (see p237).

★ **Modern Dansih architecture**

Best

- Black Diamond, p54
- Nationalbanken, p55
- New wing of Ny Carlsberg Glyptotek, p33
- Statens Museum for Kunst, p80
- Terminal Three at Copenhagen Airport, p21

★ Den Sorte Diamant (Black Diamond)

Søren Kierkegaards Plads 1, **T** 33474747. *Library Mon-Fri 1000-1900, Sat 1000-1400. Building 0800-2300 (closed on public holidays, Jun 5 and the Sat before Easter). Bus 8. Harbour Buses 901, 902. Map 3, D8, p253*

The Black Diamond, now the semi-official name for the seven-storey extension to the **Royal Library**, is situated on the waterfront across from the old library building and connected to it by a walkway. The red-brick library of 1906 and its venerable clothing of ivy is dwarfed by a bold 1999 black-granite and smoked-glass edifice that tilts severely towards the water's edge. Inside, from a sandstone floor and amidst silk-like concrete pillars a sleek escalator glides visitors up to the library of 200,000 books itself, but be sure to also use the walkway to view the reading room of the old library across the road. Back downstairs, there is a bookshop, a café named after the publication that brought Kierkegaard into print, and the Søren K restaurant (see p146) named after the philosopher. The basement houses the **National Photography Museum** which mounts changing exhibitions based on its collections; free admission. The Black Diamond is a superb example of modern Danish design, looking like a piece of black flint on a rainy day while at night it takes on the appearance of a finely cut gemstone cushioned in the black fabric of night.

★ Børsen
Børsgade. *Not open to the public. Map 3, C8, p253*

Copenhagen's old stock exchange, despite not being open to the public, is well worth a walk just to stand in the vicinity and admire the curious, almost waggish, design of the building. It took over 20 years to finish the building, under the patronage of Christian IV in the first half of the 17th century, and ranks as Europe's oldest stock exchange. It was built near the water to facilitate the unloading of cargo – the 'stock' for exchange – which was brought into the public hall that constituted the building's ground floor. What is so striking, though, is the imaginative aesthetic that shaped the exterior design and the excess of decoration so at odds with its mercantile function. The most delightful and eye-catching feature is the green copper roof and its whimsical spire composed of four plaited dragons' tails. The crowns on the summit represent Denmark, Sweden and Norway, the three trading nations whose products were sold in the hall below.

Holmens Kirke
Holmens Kanal, **T** 33136178. *Mon-Fri 0900-1400, Sat 0900-1200. Free. Map 3, C8, p253*

Across the canal from Børsen, Holmens Kirke was converted from a naval forge to a church for the navy around the time that construction work began on the stock exchange. The exterior is prosaic enough, but there are some choice sarcophagi and a carved oak altarpiece worth appreciating. And to complete an architectural tour, note the resolute dark bank building next door; the **Nationalbanken** (National Bank) designed by the famous Arne Jacobsen (see p42).

Black magic
Once a red-bricked library, the site has been transformed into one of the sleekest and most modern buildings in the city.

Nyhavn and around

This area has a twin appeal, catering to hedonists and consumers as well as museum lovers and successfully managing to do both in the unique **Museum Erotica**. Prestigious stores are to be found along **Østergade**, where Strøget begins its long, shop-laden route to Rådhuspladsen, and the network of small streets that lie to the north of Østergade are filled with specialty stores and restaurants. A more populist atmosphere characterizes the sunny side of Nyhavn, facing the eponymous canal, where a cluster of eateries draws in crowds of sightseers. Then again, around the corner from Nyhavn on stately **Bredgade**, the mood abruptly changes once again amidst the many reminders of inherited affluence. Known as **Frederiksstaden**, after King Frederik V who laid out the area in the mid-18th century, this end of the city has more than a fair share of palaces and churches plus some absorbing museums and the remains of an old fortress, the **Kastellet**. To the west of Frederiksstaden lies another royal area, this one owing its existence to Christian IV, who in the 16th century built his own castle and grounds, the much-visited **Rosenborg Slot**. Encompassing Renaissance art and contemporary porn videos, the Nyhavn and area around it is a mixed kettle of fish and all the more engaging because of this.

▸▸ See Sleeping p125, Eating and drinking p148 and Shopping p193

Sights

Nyhavn
Buses 1, 6, 9, 10, 19, 29, 31, 32, 42, 43, 350S, 650S to Kongens Nytorv. Harbour buses 901, 902. Metro Kongens Nytorv. *Map 3, A9, p253*

A canal goes down the middle, but it is only the north side of Nyhavn that has been given a Dutch makeover, transforming the restored house-fronts with an ebullient mix of colours that helps encourage gaggles of visitors to sit on the quayside and soak up the sun with their backs to a line of small boats. By walking to the end of the street, where the canal meets the open sea, it is just about possible to sense the salty ghost of Nyhavn's maritime past, for up until the end of the 1970s this area was still a sailors' hangout with a decidedly sleazy tone. At the other end of the canal, the huge anchor is a memorial to Danish seamen who died during the Second World War, and on the nearby corner of Nyhavn and Bredgade stands the **Amber Museum**. There are interesting displays of amber embedded with insects and plants from the geological past, and a shop retailing amber-related jewellery and gifts. **DFDS Canal Tours** (see p29) depart from this end of Nyhavn.

Kongens Nytorv
Map 3, A8, p253

Kongens Nytorv, the large square at the closed end of Nyhavn canal and where Strøget and other important streets converge, was renowned for its beautiful elm trees until they succumbed to Dutch elm disease a few years back. Each June the square still hosts the dancing of high school students around the statue of another dead white male called Christian (this time in Roman garb and helmet), to celebrate the passing of their final exams, and in winter a free skating rink of artificial ice is built on the square. On a cloudy, humourless day, Kongens Nytorv can resemble a public square in Ceausescu-era Bucharest due to its size and the lumbering presence of haughty edifices like the **Hôtel d'Angleterre** and **Det Kongelige Teater** (the Royal Theatre), but when the sun is out and the cafés are busy serving tired shoppers the space lightens up and it's fun to just sit and people-watch.

The Renaissance-style theatre from the 1870s dominates the physical space and culturally it packs quite a hefty punch too, combining performances of ballet, opera and drama under the one

Maritime makeover
Nyhaven was once Copenhagen's route to the sea. Today, visitors, rather than sailors, hang out on the quayside.

roof, see p186. The Dutch baroque building next to the theatre is **Charlottenborg Palace**, *www.charlottenborg-art.dk, 1000-1700, 20kr*, once a royal abode and now home to the **Royal Academy of Fine Arts**. It is worth a quick gander to admire the courtly interior. Art exhibitions are held in a building to the rear of the Charlottenborg Palace.

Upper Strøget
Map 3, B7/8, p253

Østergade, beginning at Kongens Nytorv and ending when it runs into Amagertorv at the junction with Købmagergade, is the beginning of Strøget (see p40). **Købmagergade**, also pedestrianized, is fairly indistinguishable from Strøget in its pretension to quality shopping, but the two stores with a genuine claim to fame are both on Østergade: **Illum** (see p199) and **Bang og Olufsen** (see p200). Across the street from **Illum**, it is only a few steps to **Højbro Plads** and its landmark statue of **Bishop Absalon** (see p52) Østergade's name (East Street) harks back to the Middle Ages when the city eastern gate was situated here, and like other sections of Strøget its medieval origins are revealed in the slight curvature of the street.

Museum Erotica
Købmagergade 24, **T** 33120311, www.museumerotica.dk
May-Sep, 1000-2300, Oct-Apr, 1100-2000. Adults 69kr. Buses 31, 42, 43. S-Tog and Metro, Nørreport or Kongens Nytorv. Map 3, B7, p253

Not the kind of sleazy sin-bin a sex museum could so easily masquerade as, Museum Erotica offers a spanking good time as it romps through history from Etruscan and ancient Greek times, India and the Orient, and up to modern times with displays on 1950s America and a chronicle of prostitution in Copenhagen. The visual images are not especially titillating, though the occasionally acrobatic one is more arresting, and the Shock Room has contemporary sex videos. Women, apparently, make up half the number of visitors but the choice of videos in the Shock Room is a disappointment in this respect.

Kunstindustrimuseet (Danish Museum of Decorative Art)

Bredgade 68, T 33185656, www.kunstindustrimuseet.dk
Permanent collections Tue-Fri 1300-1600, Sat-Sun 1200-1600. Special
exhibitions Tue-Fri 1000-1600, Sat-Sun 1200-1600. Adults 35kr,
children free. Buses 1, 6, 9, 29. Harbour Buses 901, 902 to Nordre
Toldbod. S-Tog, Østerport. Metro Kongens Nytorv. Map 4, G10, p255

The permanent collections at the Danish Museum of Decorative Art cover the period from the Middle Ages to 1800 and there are excellent displays of furniture, silverware, ceramics and the like. The Japanese and Chinese collections are especially superb with some exquisite Renaissance, Baroque and rococo exhibits. Special exhibitions tend to focus on Danish design and crafts of the 20th century and there should be something of interest on display at the time of your visit. Recent displays have covered Nordic jewellery, modern glassware, photography, textiles, and the work of individual artists from around the world. The museum building was originally a hospital founded in the 18th-century and a plaque in the old hospital garden records the death of Kierkegaard here in 1855. There is Danish designer furniture in the delightful café on the premises, and in the summer there is nothing more cultured than taking tea outside in the peaceful courtyard.

● *If the time available for appreciating fine arts and antiques is precious, don't be distracted by Rosenborg Slot but head for Kunstindustrimuseet instead.*

Four palaces fit for a queen
Home of Queen Magrethe II, Amalienborg Slot has four palaces, rococo monuments to statepower.

Marmorkirken (Marble Church)

Frederiksgade 4, **T** 33150144. *Mon-Thu 1000-1700, Fri-Sun
1200-1700. Dome, Mid-Jun-Aug 1300 and 1500, Sep-mid-June,
Sat-Sun 1300 and 1500. Free, dome 20kr. Buses 1, 6, 9, 29. S-Tog,
Østerport. Metro, Kongens Nytorv. Map 4, H9, p255*

The delights of Copenhagen are invariably tucked away behind
modestly small doors so there is something immediately
suspicious, confirmed when you step inside, about the jaw-
dropping pomp and glory of the Marble Church's exterior.
Designed to out-do St Peter's in Rome, the church was built for
nobility in the mid-18th century, but took well over a century to
complete because of soaring costs. The soulless interior has little
to recommend it other than providing a space for classical music
concerts between October and Easter, and for access to the dome
from where there are panoramic views across to Sweden.

● *The visual splendour of the Marble Church distracts attention
from its close neighbour, a Russian Orthodox church, whose golden
onion-shaped cupolas possess their own quieter charm.*

Amalienborg

Amalienborg, **T** 33122186, www.kulturnet.dk/homes/rosenb
*Museum, May-Oct 1000-1800, Nov-Dec and Jan-Apr, Tue-Sun
1100-1800. Closed 19-26 Dec. Adults 40kr, children 10kr. Buses 1, 6,
9,10, 29, 650S. Metro, Kongens Nytorv. Map 4, H10, p255*

Amalienborg consists of four palaces, home to Danish royalty since
1794, designed by the architect, Nicolai Eigtved, who was also
responsible for the Marble Church. The four palaces, rococo
monuments to state power, tend to exhibit the same coldness of
spirit that characterizes the church, but the octagonal cobbled
courtyard, around which they are situated, is a visitor-friendly
place, and the colourful changing of the bearskin-garbed guards
is a photogenic occasion.

A set of royal apartments constitute the museum, **De Danske Kongers Kronologiske Samling**, stuffed to the brim with fine carpets, embellished furniture, portraits of forgettable persons filling the walls, Fabergé objects and assorted trinkets. Unless specially drawn to exhibits of this kind, you may well find the nearby **Medicinsk-Historisk Museum** (Medical History Museum) to be more interesting, and with the benefit of free admission. Five minutes away from Amalienborg, head back to Bredgade and turn right to find it on the next corner, in the direction of Kunstindustrimuseet.

● *When the queen is in residence in Amalienborg (look for a raised flag), the changing of the guard is accompanied by a military band.*

Frihedsmuseet (Resistance Museum)

Churchillparken, **T** 33137714, www.natmus.dk *May-mid-Sep, Tue-Sat 1000-1600, Sun 1000-1700, Mid-Sep-Apr, Tue-Sat 1100-1500, Sun 1100-1600. Adults 30kr, children free. Wed, free. Free guided tours, Tue, Thu, Sun 1400. Buses 1, 6, 9, 19, 29. Harbour Buses 901, 902 to Nordre Toldbod. S-Tog, Østerport. Map 4, F11, p255*

Nazi Germany invaded Denmark on 9 April 1940, wanting control of the country's airfields to help establish naval bases in Norway, and the government accepted occupation in return for a pledge not to infringe Danish independence. The Resistance Museum tells the story of those who did not accept occupation, starting with socialist and communist groups in 1942, and leading to trade union activity that brought uprisings the following year and which led to martial law. An absorbing range of exhibits, with everything explained in English, range from a magnetic mine to an enigma machine, examples of home-made weapons, and one of the

! Denmark is the world's oldest kingdom. The reigning monarch, Queen Margrethe II, who lives in Copenhagen, can trace her ancestry back – over 1,000 years – to the Viking age.

Best

★ Overrated attractions

- Tivoli, p35
- Little Mermaid, p68
- Strøget, p40
- Rosenborg Slot, p68
- Amalienborg, p65

aluminium 5-øre coins introduced in 1941 that has a hammer marked over the 5 to turn it into the hammer and sickle of the USSR. Most poignant are the preserved execution stakes where 102 rebel Danes paid the ultimate price, and there is a good exhibition on how ordinary Danes saved the lives of 7,000 of their Jewish fellow citizens by spontaneously whisking them away to Sweden when news was leaked of their intended fate.

● *There is a good outdoor café with tables looking out on parkland and water.*

Gefion Springvandet (Gefion Fountain)

Amaliegade. *Buses 1, 6, 9,19, 29. Harbour Buses 901, 902 to Nordre Toldbod. S-Tog, Østerport. Map 4, F11, p255*

From the Resistance Museum it is a short walk to **St Alban's Church** and the adjoining Gefion Springvandet, an extraordinary statue that compares with the one of Frederik V in Amalienborg for sheer size. It was built in the first decade of the 20th century by Anders Bundgaard thanks to the largesse of the Carlsberg Foundation. In Nordic mythology, a king of Sweden promised the goddess Gefion the possession of as much land as she could plough in a night. What he didn't allow for was Gefion's ability to transform her four sons into oxen, who between them carved out a land mass that was hurled into the sea to form Danish Zealand. The statue is certainly eye-catching, adding to the mystery of how on earth the miniscule Den Lille Havfrue (the Little Mermaid) managed to upstage it.

Den Lille Havfrue (Little Mermaid)

Langelinie. Buses 1, 6, 9. Harbour Buses 901, 902 to Nordre Toldbod. S-Tog, Østerport. Map 4, D11, p255

The Little Mermaid is Copenhagen's most recognizable media image but seeing it for real can be a let down – the only thing that is striking about it is its inconsequentiality. Cynics think this goes a long way towards explaining why it has been vandalized three times, plus two decapitations (a third attempt never succeeded but it suffered an amputation). The bronze figure was commissioned by Carl Jacobsen, the beer magnate, in 1909 after he was moved by a performance of an opera based on Hans Christian Andersen's story of a mermaid who fell in love with a human prince. A compulsory stop on most guided tours of the city, and with cruise vessels berthing up the road at Langelinie Pier, the unprepossessing statue perched on a granite boulder attracts an unwarranted amount of attention – but you may still feel you have to see it for yourself. Around 1800 on the evening before 1 May, Finns in Denmark cap the mermaid to celebrate the arrival of spring and sell a special drink called Vappu.

Rosenborg Slot (Rosenborg Castle)

Øster Voldgade, T 33153286, www.kulturnet.dk/homes/rosenb Jun-Aug 1000-1700, Sep and May 1000-1600, Oct 1100-1500, Nov-Apr Tue-Sun 1100-1400. Adults 60kr, children 10kr. The free plan gives a bare description, but the 25kr-guide is needed to properly sort out what's what amongst all the clutter. Buses 5, 10, 14, 16, 31, 42, 43. S-Tog and Metro, Nørreport. Map 4, G6/H6, p254

The castle was originally built in 1606 as a country residence for Christian IV, and over the following 30 years developed into the

Dizzy in Denmark
Neat urban living – the capital's rooftops as seen from the Rådhuset Tower.

Sound familiar?

Elections at the end of 2001 saw a right-wing shift among sections of the population, resulting in a conservative-liberal alliance which lost little time in pushing forward the anti-immigration and anti-Muslim policies of the Danish People's Party. Foreigners sentenced to six months or more in prison will have to wait 10 years before receiving permanent residency, refugees will lose their current right to 'fitting accommodation' after leaving an asylum centre, access to the welfare system for asylum seekers and immigrants will be restricted, tests in language and culture will be tightened up for would-be citizens, and faster deportations of illegal immigrants will be introduced.

Dutch Renaissance castle that you see today. Always the favourite abode of Christian IV, he chose to die here and arrived outside at the moat in the middle of winter, having been carried by sleigh from Frederiksborg. In the years before his death, though, Christian filled his toy castle with a vast assortment of art and non-art, so much so that the love of minimalism amongst Danes might make sense as a healthy reaction to such pathological excess. To be fair, the kings that came after Christian added their own loot, and the final result is a surfeit of Flemish tapestries, furniture (lacquered, mahogany, silver), chandeliers, gilded bronze, glass and porcelain cabinets, jewel boxes, writing tables, mirrors, marble busts, paintings by the score (bare breasts and bums are a favourite subject on the ground floor ceiling), couches, clocks, toys, jewellery, cameos, beakers, swords, guns... The basement treasury is chock-full of jewel boxes, forks and spoons, snuff boxes and trinkets all in gold and all taking second place to the Sword of State and the crown jewels.

Kongens Have (Royal Gardens)

May-Aug 0700-2200, Apr and Sep 0700-2100, Feb-mid-Mar and Oct 0700-1800, mid-Mar-end-Mar 0700-2000, Nov-Jan 0700-1700. Hercules Pavilion, May-Oct 1000-2000. Buses 5, 10, 14, 16, 31, 42, 43. S-Tog and Metro, Nørreport. *Map 4, H7, p255*

At weekends and whenever the sun is out, the spacious grounds of Rosenborg Royal Gardens are deservedly popular with Copenhageners. Planned in Renaissance style at the same time as Rosenborg Slot, while also functioning as the castle's vegetable gardens, a stroll or a picnic here makes an exhilarating change after trawling through the cavernous gloom of the castle's interior. Tidy to the point of being manicured, there are diverting statues to ponder over and a restored Renaissance garden with a summerhouse and historical roses. The imaginative playground will appeal to children and the 18th-century Hercules Pavilion has a good café serving refreshments and light meals.

Davids Samling

Kronprinsessegade 30, T 33734949. Thu-Sun and Tue 1300-1600, Wed 1000-1600. Free. Buses 10, 43. S-Tog and Metro, Nørreport. Map 4, H8, p255

Davids was a private Danish collector, he died in 1960, and his possessions are now open to the public in the house where he lived. Most of what you see on the lower floors is a fairly unexciting selection of fine arts from Denmark, France and England, but if you work your way past the Chippendale, silverware and porcelain there is ample reward in the collection of Islamic art on the fourth floor. This is the largest such collection in Scandinavia and there are superb examples of glassware, textiles, ceramics and jewellery, as well as a large collection of holy texts from the last seven centuries.

Vesterbro and Frederiksberg

*Although the area immediately behind the railway station has plenty of hotels and sex shops, **Vesterbro** is not tourist land and a stroll down **Istedgade** offers a window on contemporary Copenhagen. In the 19th century, the city authorities came to regard the area as suitable ground for a working-class ghetto and thousands of tiny apartments were crammed into unsanitary housing blocks. Recent renovation work is gentrifying parts of Vesterbro, and an ethnic dimension is added by immigrants from Asia and Africa who settled in the area when rents were low. The result is a pleasing mix of people and classes, which is more than can be found along the tree-lined boulevards and elegant gardens of snooty **Frederiksberg** further to the west. While Istedgade sums up Vesterbro, the best approach to Frederiksberg is by way of stately **Frederiksberg Allé** which branches off Vesterbrogade and terminates at the main entrance to a grand park and gardens, one of which jumps into life in the summer when hosting gigs for the city's **jazz festival**. Places of interest in Vesterbro and Frederiksberg are as diverse as the areas themselves, including a porcelain factory and a planetarium.*

▸▸ *See Sleeping p127 and Eating and drinking p153*

Sights

Istedgade and Vesterbrogade
Bus 16 (Istedgade), 6,28,550S (Vesterbrogade). Map 3, D2/E2, p252

These two streets, running sort-of parallel from **Central Station** westwards, are Vesterbro's main arteries, but they differ markedly in character. Vesterbrogade begins at Rådhuspladsen, passing the side of Tivoli before metamorphosing into a prime shopping street shortly after passing the *Radisson SAS Royal Hotel*. It is a lively street with a variety of places to eat and shops that range from an all-purpose department store, with a supermarket at ground level, to a host of smaller retail stores.

Strolling westwards along Istedgade throws up Copenhagen's social character like stratified layers of geological time. To begin with, to the rear of Central Station, there is evidence of what passes for the city's low life, but being Denmark it is all perfectly civilized and visitors have nothing to fear from huddled individuals exchanging little packets and cans of beer. Within a couple of hundred metres of walking down Istedgade, three-star hotels begin to predominate, and as quickly again the street gives way to sex shops as a seedy tawdriness threatens to, but never actually succeeds, in defining the atmosphere. The human landscape becomes an interesting mix, distinctly non-bourgeois, ethnic and semi-gentrified, with no surfeit of Danes with glacial good looks to make you feel inadequate. Istedgade terminates at Enghave Plads and a small park, where anarchists gather on 1 May to start their feeder procession that joins the trade union marches through the city.

Københavns Bymuseum (City Museum)

Vesterbrogade 59, **T** 33210772, www.bymuseum.dk *May-Sep, Wed-Mon 1000-1600, Oct-Apr, Wed-Mon 1300-1600. Film 1115, 1245, 1415 (worth seeing). Adults 20kr, children free. Free on Fri. Buses 6, 28, 550S. Map 2, E12, p251*

The City Museum, a series of well-presented exhibition rooms organized chronologically and with everything in English, offers a more enjoyable way to engage with Copenhagen's past than plodding through a dull history book. There is plenty to see, well meriting the admission price, including a large model of the city in 1660 and a modest exhibition on Kierkegaard that includes his writing desk and the 25-minute-film in English. The museum is housed in a mansion built by the Royal Shooting Society in 1787 and its banquet room, which stands as renovated a century later, is now a very pleasant café serving drinks, cakes, beer and wine.

Kirstenberg – probably the least famous lager in the world

If the wife of JC (Jacob Christian) Jacobsen had given birth to a daughter instead of a son called Carl, would the famous beer now be known as Kirstenberg or Karenberg? Maybe not, daughters having the wrong gender to run a brewery in the 19th century. Carl's grandfather, Christen Jacobsen (1773-1835) the father of JC, was a small brewer in the city, but when JC heard of a new style of brewing Bavarian beers he headed off to Germany and returned with a pot of lager yeast in his hat box. He decided to move production of his new beer to a better site on high ground near Frederiksberg. He named it Carlsberg (Carl's hill), although relations between father and son would later sour – they refused to speak to one another for years – and Carl Jacobsen went on to establish his own brewery, separated by a wall from his father's setup. It was Carl who, growing even more fabulously rich than his father, founded the Ny (new) Carlsberg Foundation, as opposed to the original Foundation created by his father. Hence the name of the art gallery, the Ny Carlsberg Glyptotek (see p33).

Tycho Brahe Planetarium
Gammel Kongevej 10, **T** 33121224, www.tycho.dk *Mon, Fri-Sun 1030-2100, Tue and Thu 0930-2100, Wed 0945-2100. Adults 85kr, children 65kr. Buses 1, 14, 16. Map 3, D2, p252 See also p220*

The admission price is a bit steep, what you are paying for is the experience of an Omnimax 1000m2 dome screen. There is a good choice of film topics – from dolphins to 3D technology, the human body, Antarctica, caves, ancient Egypt – with headphones for those in Danish.

★ Radisson SAS Royal Hotel
Hammerischsgade 1, **T** 33426000. *Buses 6, 28, 550S.* *Map 3, D3, p252*

The unprepossessing glass tower of the hotel (see p127) that the world-renowned Arne Jacobsen (see p42) designed remains a city landmark if only by virtue of its height. Voted the ugliest building in the city when completed in 1960, the aesthetic appeal of what became the 'landmark of the Jet Age' remains evasive and Jacobsen's interior design attracted both derision and praise. Critics could not get their heads around his combination of a minimalist style with loosely organic forms and a strict functionalism, dismissing his approach as outlandishly avant garde, while others admired the simple elegance and subdued luxury. The lobby has been preserved unchanged, still furnished with the famous Swan and Egg chairs designed for the hotel. Here, too, can be seen the curved staircase, cutting-edge style at a time when technical skills were carried to their extreme to create such a slight structure, and the adjoining bar area comes complete with Jacobsen-designed ashtrays. Room 606 has been retained exactly as it was first designed and if you have a special interest, or ask nicely, you may be allowed to view it.

Carlsberg Brewery Visitor Centre
Gamle Carlsberg Vej 11, **T** 33271314. *Mon-Fri 1000-1600. Free.* *Buses 6, 18.* *Map 2, H7, p251*

Catching a bus avoids a walk up Pile Allé, though knowing there is a free drink at the end of your visit to the centre helps the flagging spirit on a hot day. You don't get to see the actual brewery, a self-guided tour leads visitors around mildly-interesting displays on the history and technology of brewing the famous lager, but when passing the Elephant Gate note the decorative swastikas. At one time swastikas were seen as a symbol of quality and cleanliness and Carlsberg adopted them as such, and they could be seen on bottles until the Second World War. To find out more about the history of Carlsberg and its founding brewer, the benevolent Christen Jacobsen, there is also the separate Carlsberg Museum.

Bakkehusmuseet (Bakkehus Museum)

Rahbeks Allé 23, **T** 33314362, www.bakkehusmuseet.dk *Wed-Thu, Sat-Sun 1100-1500. Adults 10kr. Buses 6, 18, 550S. Map 2, G8, p251*

Situated between Frederiksberg Have and Carlsberg Brewery, the Bakkehus Museum pays homage to the intellectual culture of Denmark's Golden Age (1780-1830) and its sense of style. The museum was once the private home of Knud Lyne Rahbek and his wife Kamma, at the start of the 19th century, and is now home to a catholic collection of cultural bric-a-brac. Knud Lyne was a professor of literature and became famous for the literary salon he hosted in his home, Hans Christian Andersen being a regular visitor. The fact that today Bakkehusmuseet attracts only a modest number of visitors helps allow the place to maintain that sense of stylish repose that is associated with the Golden Age.

Royal Copenhagen Welcome Centre

Smallegad 47, **T** 38149297, www.royalcopenhagen.com *Tours Mon-Fri 1000, 1100, 1300, 1400. Shop Mon-Fri 0900-1730, Sun 0900-1400. Adults 25kr. Buses 1,14, 39, 100S. Map 2, B5, p250*

The famous Danish porcelain company moved here in 1884, over a century after its foundation, and the guided tours are interesting enough to get you hooked on starting a china collection. While the renowned **Flora Danica** design is beyond most people's crockery budget, the factory shop sells more affordable pieces (see p202) and old **Royal Copenhagen** is sold in antique shops around town (see p195).

On two wheels
In Copenhagen it would appear that almost everyone owns and rides a bicycle.

Frederiksberg Have (Frederiksberg Park)

T 33926300. *May-Aug 0700-2200, closing earlier in other months. Chinese Island, May-Sep, Sun 1400-1600. Rowing boats Jun-Aug, Mon-Fri 1000-1700, Sat-Sun 1200-1800. Free. Buses 1, 6, 14, 18, 28. Map 2, D6, p250*

A conversion job at the end of the 18th century turned the expansive landscape of Frederiksberg Park from baroque to romantic, hence the amalgam of lakes and canals, a Chinese pavilion on a small island, plus a neoclassical Temple of Apis for a touch of ancient Greek enlightenment. Always a popular escape for apartment-living Copenhageners, Frederiksberg Park offers itself as an ideal picnic spot in between visiting the brewery, Royal Copenhagen factory and the zoo (see p219).

Frederiksberg Slot (Frederiksberg Castle)

Roskildevej 32, **T** 36162244. *Guided tours 1100, last Sat of month. Adults 25kr. Buses 6, 18, 28, 550S. Map 2, D6, p250*

The yellow palace building on top of the hill at the southern end of the park is Frederiksberg Castle, a summer pad for the royals for around 150 years after Frederik IV had the place built in the early 18th century. Frederiksberg Allé was built as a private road for the royal entourage to reach the stately residence, and you have to imagine the fine view which the palace would have commanded looking east across the city towards Sweden. Tours of the interior are infrequent so you may have to content yourself with admiring the fine simplicity of the exterior, originally designed to imitate the grand Italian villas that so impressed Frederik on one of his European jaunts. The building was modified by subsequent royals, most notably by Christian VI, who had the two side wings added in the middle of the 18th century. The monthly tour inside the building is worth considering because the decorative stucco and painted ceilings have been wonderfully well preserved and, unlike

Rosenborg Slot, do not overwhelm to the point of overkill. The palace now belongs to the Ministry of Defence and houses the Royal Military Academy.

● *It's easy to confuse the park and castle of Frederiksberg with the park and castle of Frederiksborg, which is outside Copenhagen in the town of Hillerød, see p114.*

Around the Three Lakes

With parts of central Copenhagen a tad too manicured and mono-cultural for its own good, the workaday, multi-cultural feel of **Nørrebro** *provides a healthy antidote. As in Vesterbro, young professionals are gentrifying the area with voguish cafés, bars and clothes shops, but it is the Palestinians, Turks, Asians and other immigrants who bring a tang of cosmopolitanism to the street life. Nørrebro is a good hunting ground for clothes and Danish bric-a-brac of the sort not found back home, while the* **Workers' (Arbejdermuseet) and Police museums** *acknowledge in their different ways the area's proletarian identity. Every 1 May, a colourful procession of workers wends its way through Nørrebro to the sound of brass instruments. Also in the neighbourhood is* **Assistens Kirkegård**, *a calm oasis for a rest or picnic and as far from being a gloomy cemetery as anyone could wish. Across the bridge from Nørrebro, on the city side of the lakes, where the* **Botanic Gardens** *provide another green space, there are two top-notch art galleries. One is the esteemed* **Danish National Gallery** *with major works of European art, while tucked away behind it is the lesser-known but highly rewarding* **Den Hirschsprungske Samling**, *a treasure trove of Danish art from the last two centuries.*

▸▸ *See Sleeping p133 and Eating and drinking p157*

★ **Galleries**

Best

- Statens Museum for Kunst, p80
- Louisiana, p101
- Den Hirschsprungske Samling, p81
- Davids Samling, p71
- Arken Museum for Moderne Kunst, p116

 Sights

★ Statens Museum for Kunst

Sølvgade 48, **T** 33748494, www.smk.dk *Tue-Sun 1000-1700, Wed 1000-2000, closed on public holidays, Easter Monday, Whit Monday, 23-5 Dec, 30 Dec-1 Jan. Adults 50kr. Free Wed. During Jul and Aug there are free guided tours in English at weekends, see website for details, and tickets are available up to half an hour in advance. Buses 10, 14, 40, 42, 43, 184, 185, 150S, 72E, 79E, 173E. S-Tog Østerport, Nørreport. Metro, Nørreport.* Map 4, G7, p255 See also 219

Although the Danish National Gallery is not up there with the world class leaders, you may well find yourself planning a second visit because of the rich variety of Danish and non-Danish work on show. Seven centuries of art are represented, from the Italian Renaissance to modern art, and the free miniguide with concise, intelligent comment is available with your ticket, and it serves to highlight two dozen paintings that reflect the quality and variety of the permanent collections. Focus is also given to the changing 'exhibit of the month', (see the website for details), and top marks to the gallery's policy of mounting special displays that address the works of one artist or, more interestingly, a particular theme that may have a topical relevance. Look out, too, for international touring exhibitions which often use the gallery. They can stay for months and can justify a visit in their own right. There is a children's section to the gallery, an exemplary bookshop and a stylish café (see p157).

(see p157).

Den Hirschsprungske Samling

Stockholmsgade 20, **T** 35420336, www.hirschsprung.dk *Thu-Mon 1100-1600, Wed 1100-2100. Adults 25kr. Free Wed.* Buses 10, 14, 40, 42, 43, 72E, 79E, 150S, 184,185. S-Tog, Østerport, Nørreport. Metro, Nørreport. *Map 4, F6, p254*

Heinrich Hirschsprung (1836-1908) was a tobacco magnate who built up a personal collection of Danish art and later donated it to the nation on condition that a suitable building was built to house the paintings. The result is a house with a series of interconnecting rooms that function as small galleries and, although some of the exhibits could charitably be called mediocre (like no 443 in room 19), there are some real delights that will surprise the visitor. The best-known painter of Denmark's Golden Age was and still is CW Eckersberg (1783-1853) and his fresh concern with the everyday world influenced the work of students of his like Christen Købke and Wilhelm Bendz, both of whom are represented here with accomplished works in room 2. Eckersberg studied and worked in Paris and Rome before returning to Copenhagen as Professor of Painting in the Academy of Fine Arts and earning commissions from the city's emerging middle-class merchants, as evidenced in his *Portrait of Mrs Schmidt* (no 112, room 1). The glum Mrs Schmidt is offset by the bourgeois voyeurism of his *Woman before a Mirror* (no 123, room 1), which plays cleverly with concealment, while Dreyer's *Barrow on the Island of Brandsø* (no 100, room 5) openly reveals all, past and present, in a Danish summer landscape of lush freshness. A complete contrast is found in the haunting landscape that forms the background of Nielsen's *The Blind Girl* (no 338, room 19), a startling and arresting portrayal of blindness. There are a number of paintings of couples that

Form and content

Two of Copenhagen's most renowned galleries, the Ny Carlsberg Glyptotek (see p33) and the Statens Museum for Kunst (see p80) have risen to the challenge of commissioning design extensions that aspire to being works of art in their own right. The new wing of the Glyptotek, which should be viewed from outside on the street as well as inside the museum, strives to integrate itself with the classical mode of the original building without sacrificing its minimalist principles. Shimmering white surfaces reflect the natural light from the glass roof, creating an airy composure that merges modernism with classicism, and the successful style of the Danish architect, Henning Larsen, can also be appreciated at the airport's Terminal Three for which he is also responsible. The architectural world waits impatiently to see the city's new opera house for which Larsen has also been commissioned.

The 1998 extension to the Statens Museum for Kunst, designed by Anna Maria Indrio, is certainly visually stunning as you walk into it from the main foyer to be confronted by a canvas of natural greenery (a public park) behind a vast glass wall, turning the park view into a giant living painting, with light pouring in from the glass roof and the sides.

Another example of form merging with content is to be found in the Arken Museum for Moderne Kunst (see p116) in the Ishøj suburb of Copenhagen.

throw up interesting comparisons, from the voluptuous decadence of Zahrtmann's court painting in room 13 to the muted symbolism of Ring's *Spring* (no 402, room 19) and the silent social criticism of Henningsen's *The Murder of a Child* (no 154, room 12). A favourite of many is Anna Ancher's *The Maid in the Kitchen* (no 7, room 20), perhaps because of the way it suggests one of Vermeer's Dutch interiors, and *Spring* by the Pre-Raphaelites-inspired Harald Slott-Møller. Given that most of what you see will be unfamiliar, and the lack of details attached to the canvases, the booklet that focuses on 20 of the collection's major works is well worth purchasing.

Botanisk Have (Botanical Gardens)

Gothersgade 128, T 35322240, www.botanic-garden.ku.dk
May-Sep 0800-1800, Oct-Apr 0830-1600. Palmhouse Tue-Sun 1000-1500. Cactus and orchid greenhouses Wed, Sat, Sun, 1300-1500. Free. Museum Jun-Aug, Mon-Fri 1300-1530, Sat-Sun 1300-1430. Adults 50kr. Buses 5, 7, 14, 16, 24, 40, 43, 84, 384. S-Tog and Metro, Nørreport. Map 4, G5, p254

Creatively occupying what was once the city's northern fortifications, the present Botanic Gardens were laid out in 1871 as a resource for the botany department of Copenhagen University. Part of the defensive moat was remodelled as a lake and the rock garden utilizes the old ramparts, and pathways weave their way around the garden areas allowing visitors to wander about the grounds. Some 25,000 specimens from 13,000 species are growing in the Gardens, half of which are not the kind found growing in ordinary gardens, and a small shop just inside the entrance on Øster Farimagsgade (the other entrance is at the corner of Gothersgade and Øster Voldgade) sells a selection of seeds of the more uncommon ones. The palmhouse, modelled on London's Kew Gardens, is an atmospheric steamhouse of giant palms and lily-clad ponds and, next door, the cactus and orchid green-houses are home to some 1,000 species of cactus and half that number of orchids. Behind the palmhouse the Café Paradisfuglen (Bird of Paradise) serves pastries, ice creams, beer, wine and sandwiches. The summer-only museum is near the entrance at the corner of Gothersgade and Øster Voldgade.

Geologisk Museum (Geological Museum)

Øster Voldgade 5, **T** 35322345, www.geological-museum.dk
*Tue-Sun 1300-1400. Adults 25kr, children 10kr. Free Wed. Buses 5, 10,
14, 16, 31, 42, 43, 184, 185, 150S, 350S. S-Tog and Metro, Nørreport.
Map 4, G6, p254*

The Geological Museum is not as dull as you might imagine and
while it may take a special interest to get excited by the vast array
of minerals, there are interesting exhibits to be found, like the 150
million-year-old imprint of a jellyfish and the fossilized footprint
trod in volcanic ash some 250,000 years ago. The collection of
meteorites from Greenland is especially impressive – is it possible
that Peter Høeg first got his idea for *Miss Smilla's Feeling for Snow*
(see p237) from a visit here?

Arbejdermuseet (Workers' Museum)

Rømersgade 22, **T** 33933388, www.arbejdermuseet.dk *Jan-Jun,
Tue-Sat 1000-1600, Jul-Oct 1000-1600, Nov-Dec 1000-1600. Adults
50kr, children 30kr. Buses 5, 14, 16, 31, 40, 42, 43,173, 184, 185, 350S.
S-Tog and Metro, Nørreport. Map 4, H5, p254*

The worthy Workers' Museum is beginning to look a little tired,
and space becomes cramped as so many aspects of working-class
life are exhibited in the small rooms, but partly as a result the right
kind of atmosphere prevails for a visual history of deprivation and
inequality. From the fading colours of the artefacts emerge
glimpses of the hard life endured by workers and their families –
like the table turned upside down to form a child's bed – and
noticeably absent are products of the famous Danish designers.
A personal story is told of the Sorenson family who moved into a
new flat in 1915. Their apartment and its contents were donated
to the museum by a daughter who occupied it until she moved
into a nursing home in 1990. Traditional Danish food and drinks
are available in the period café in the basement of the museum.

Israels Plads and Ørsteds Parken
Map 3, A4, p252 See also p203

Israels Plads, once the site of the city's main vegetable market, still a market atmosphere with stalls selling fruit, vegetables and flowers and discount-seeking shoppers. Adjoining the square, **Ørsteds Parken** is named after the Danish physicist Hans Christian Ørsteds who discovered electromagnetism. There is a summer café in the middle of the park, while back at Israels Plads on Saturdays a **flea market** springs to life, with some of the city's antique shops setting up stalls to retail their less costly merchandise.

Assistens Kirkegård
Kapelvej. *Free. Buses 5, 16,18, 350S. S-Tog and Metro, Nørreport. Map 4, F1, p254*

Far from being soul mates, Hans Christian Andersen and Søren Kierkegaard nevertheless found a common resting place in death, both being buried in Assistens Kirkegård. Not the only famous figures in the cemetery, the Danish winner of the Nobel Prize for physics, Niels Bohr, and the Kansas jazz tenorist Ben Webster are also here. These famous graves are signposted. However, there is more to Assistens Kirkegård than morbid lists of the dead famous, as seen by the way Copenhageners treat it as a public park, picnicking and sunbathing in the open spaces under the magnolia trees. The civic authorities haven't gone to the extent of placing benches amid the tombs, but it is easy to find a spot to sit and relax.

Politihistorisk Museum (Police Museum)
Fælledvej 20, **T** 35368888. *Tue, Thu and Sun 1100-1600. Adults 25kr. Buses 3, 5, 16, 350S. Map 4, F6, p254*

Although the amount of information in English in the Police Museum is not tremendous, the exhibits tell their own graphic stories in what was the city's first proper police station when it opened over a century ago. As well as old police badges, uniforms and motorbikes, there are well-presented displays on various facets of the city's criminal past that do not pull any punches when it comes to portraying the more unsavoury aspects of violent crime and violent punishment.

Sankt Hans Torv
Buses 3, 5, 16, 350S. Map 4, E2, p254

Just up the road from the museum at Sankt Hans Torv, a large junction where half a dozen streets converge, a rather different class of citizens to those who feature in the Police Museum come out to role play around the chic cafés in the summer months. Nørrebro's renaissance began when canny young professionals started taking advantage of the neighbourhood's low rents and before long a number of bars and two cafés, the now famous Sebastopol and Pussy Galore's Flying Circus (see p175), emerged to help service their relatively prosperous lifestyle. When the sun comes out, so too do the tables, chairs and parasol heaters of the cafés and the square becomes a lively social venue. Around the corner is the newly opened four-screen Empire cinema and one of Copenhagen's better-known nightclubs, Rust (see p176).

Blågårdsgade
Buses 5,16, 350S. Map 4, G2, p254

Pedestrianized Blågårdsgade, the second street on your left off **Nørrebrogade** after crossing the bridge from the city centre, is probably the most interesting street in the neighbourhood. Besides its low-key boutiques retailing affordable designer wear (p199) and off-beat eateries (p157) that make those on Sankt Hans Torv seem bourgeois, there is a gratifying mix of people cutting across class and colour lines. Palestinians rub shoulders with south

Asians, young non-mainstream professionals with anarchists, and half way down the street there is a large square, **Blågårds Plads**, with a playground and benches.

Fælled Park
Buses 1, 3, 42, 43, 184, 185, 150S. Map 4, B4, p254 See also p187

North of the lakes and to the west of Nørrebro lies the ample space of Fælled Park and, abutting it, the 40,000-seat **National Stadium** (Parken Stadium). The park was established in 1900 as an open space for the enjoyment of working people and so makes an appropriate venue for the festival that unfolds when the 1 May marchers reach their terminus in the park. There is a skateboard arena and open-air swimming pool within the park, playgrounds for children and a pleasant open-air café and restaurant. Michael Frayn's play *Copenhagen* records how crucial conversations took place in the park between the Danish physicist Niels Bohr and his German friend the physicist Heisenberg over the Nazi's ability to manufacture an atomic bomb.

Zoologisk Museum (Zoological Museum)
Universitetsparken 15, **T** 35321001, www.zoologiskmuseum.dk
Tue-Sun 1100-1700. Adults 25kr, children 10kr. Buses 18, 24, 43, 150S, 184, 185. Map 4, A2, p254

Not just a great place for children, the Zoological Museum has a wide appeal and its new exhibition – From Mammoth Steppe to Cultural Steppe – tells an exciting tale of zoological history from 20,000 years ago to the present. Interestingly too, the museum does not restrict itself to the kind of animal life that city dwellers rarely encounter and a diorama comes alive with non-human urban life. As well as all this, there is the usual array of stuffed animals from around the world, some fairly impressive stuffed walruses and the skeleton of a bowhead whale some 14 m long.

The grass is always greener
Christiania came into existence over 30 years ago when hippies, activists and others moved into the area to create an alternative way of living.

Christiania and around

*Christiania on the **island of Christianshavn**, much more than a social laboratory in alternative living, is a bustling and buzzing venue when the restaurants, cafés and stalls are teeming with patrons. The place fascinates Danes as much as foreigners and the guided tour is recommended as a quick introduction to this multi-faceted community that mixes anarchists with hard-nosed dealers, and canny careerists with 21st-century hippies. By reboarding bus no 8 from near the entrance to Christiania you travel north to **Holmen**, a disused naval station area that is now witnessing an imaginative transformation of naval buildings into homes, offices and centres for art schools and other institutions. Holmen has no specific attractions, but the industrial architecture, like the crane used to raise oak masts onto sailing vessels, is evocative and recalls the era when Greenland and Iceland were colonial possessions and Denmark ruled the waves, of the North Atlantic anyway. The same atmosphere pervades parts of **upper Strandgade**, the main street running off to the left as you come over Knippelsbro Bridge to Christianshavn. Home to a community of Greenlanders, Christianshavn provides the setting for the opening scenes of* Miss Smilla's Feeling for Snow *(see p237).*

▸ *See Eating and drinking p159 and Tours p30*

Prinsessegade, **T** 32956507, www.chistiania.org *Bus 8. Metro, Christianshavn. To get to Christiania in a hurry: take the metro or bus 8 from outside the* Thai Airways *building on Rådhuspladsen or, exiting Central Station on the Tivoli side, turn right for the bus stop where the 8 also stops. Whether walking down Prinsessegade from the metro station, or alighting from the no 8 bus which stops near the main entrance on the same street don't use the entrance directly by the bus stop, walk back about 100 m and take the first entrance on the left. Map 1, F13, p249*

◉ Sights

Pusher Street
Map 3, C12, p253

Your very first impression of Christiania can be a dismal one. A makeshift look to the entrance area and a few down-and-outs hanging about don't make for an auspicious start, but it all livens up considerably once you walk through and find yourself at the head of Pusher Street. Along this street and running off it on both sides are cafés, bars, restaurants and stalls, and the first street on the right leads to Loppen, a long building with the *Spiseloppen* restaurant (see p160) and a music venue. Pusher Street is infamous for its stalls (see p204) retailing soft drugs because the smoking of cannabis is not legal in Denmark. As in parts of England, the police are generally tolerant to non-dealers but it is only in Christiania that dealers get away with openly displaying and selling their gear and only here that smokers can enjoy the habit without looking over their shoulder. Hard drugs are strictly not available for a mix of practical and idealistic reasons. The dope dealers run private businesses and run the risk of having their stock confiscated during a police raid so they don't want to attract any more attention from the authorities than they receive already; hence their prohibition on taking photographs on Pusher Street. Note, too, that the police have the power to arrest drug users within Denmark, just as their counterparts do back home when visitors go through customs.

! The name Christiania comes from the island upon which it is situated, Christianshavn. The name of the island comes from Christian – the name of any number of departed Danish kings.

★ Vor Frelsers Kirke (Church of Our Saviour)

Sankt Annægade, **T** 32572998, www.vorfrelserskirke.dk *Church 0900-1700, free. Tower Apr-Aug 1100-1630, Sep-Mar 1100-1530 and closed between Nov and Mar. Adults 20kr. Buses 8. Metro, Christianshavn. Map 3, D10, p253*

The Church of Our Saviour was completed in 1696 and the grand Dutch Baroque style of the interior continues to dazzle when light pours in through the high windows. The altar was designed by a Swede in a Rome-inspired Baroque style, centred with a golden sun spreading light on the angels who frisk playfully in its rays, but the Lutheran influence keeps the ornate embellishments to a minimum. The massive church organ was not finished until 1700 and while it looks as if it might be supported on the backs of two stucco elephants, large iron brackets are doing this job. The real attraction of the church is its 1752 spiral tower, built in pine and covered with copper, with a whacky external staircase that twists around the tower to the top. Above you, as you stand on the highest and narrowest point of the stairs is a gilded globe on which stands a flag-bearing figure. A popular legend says that the Danish architect Laurids de Thurah committed suicide by jumping off the tower when he realized the staircase wound to the right instead of the left. A good story that could be used to hold many an architect to account but actually not true; de Thurah died in poverty seven years after the tower was completed.

Orlogsmuseet (Royal Danish Naval Museum)

Overgaden Oven Vandet 58, **T** 32546363, www.orlogsmuseet.dk *Tue-Sun 1200-1600. Adults 30kr, children 20kr. Buses 2, 8, 9, 28, 31, 37, 350S. Map 3, D10, p253*

Orlogsmuseet is worth a gander on a wet day though anyone with an interest in nautical affairs will revel in the collection of model ships that date back to the 17th century, the naval artillery,

★ **Vor Frelsers Kirke**
*The spiral staircase is the highlight of a trip to this church – though
some would have you believe the low point in the architect's career.*

The polis and the politics

The free town of Christiania came into existence over 30 years ago, when hippies, activists and others began moving into a site of abandoned military buildings and set about creating an alternative way of living. An alternative newspaper had run a story about disused army barracks and how suitable they would be as a squat, triggering off a mini-exodus of the homeless. Over the years, Christiania has experienced some tumultuous encounters with state authorities, from exasperated officials demanding taxes to invasion by brigades of riot-suited police. Now an official "social experiment", Christiania has become a major attraction for visitors intrigued by the prospect of an alternative lifestyle flourishing in the heart of a modern bourgeois state. Somewhere between 650 and 1,000 people work or live in Christiania, in homes they have mostly designed and built themselves, and free of government taxes though water and electricity is paid for. More so than in the polis of ancient classical Athens, government is fully democratic, and all major decisions are reached at open meetings to which everyone living in Christiania is invited. When a general meeting is in progress, the shops and cafés close down and discussion of items on the agenda continue until a consensus is reached. Decisions are not made on the basis of voting and, consequently, some

nautical instruments and assorted paraphernalia. The hands-on bit involves being inside a replica submarine with sound effects. Downstairs among old artillery there is an eating area for picnic lunches, and hot drinks are available.

Orlogsmuseet is not the only reminder of Christianshavn's naval role in history and the area's specialist **Burmeister & Wain**

decisions are not quickly arrived at. The town is broken down into 15 administrative and autonomous districts that hold their own monthly meetings, and contact groups are formed by district representatives as and when the need arises.

Politically, Christiania is not more homogenous than the Athenian polis. Only about 20-25% of the residents are what might loosely be called anarchists and they share living space with citizens of all political persuasions. Conservatives live in Christiania, cycle off to work in the city wearing suits and have little truck with the more public face of Christiania. There are mixed feelings about the presence of the drug pushers and their role in the town has been hotly debated on more than one occasion. The most interesting and genuinely alternative districts are the anarchist ones and even here there is a range of opinion among the mix of older, traditional libertarians and direct-action militants. There are a small number of anarchist collectives that share everything in common and some refuse to use electricity in their endeavour to live outside of the state. Mainstream Danes look on with bemused toleration, a poll in 1996 showed over 60% of the country's population agreed that Christiania should be preserved and 20% wanted the place closed down permanently.

Museum, a museum dedicated to the diesel engine, is named after a shipbuilding company that had large shipyards here.

Under German occupation in the Second World War the shipyards were used to make U-boat engines and for this reason, searly in 1943, became the target for the first Allied air raid on Copenhagen.

Arkitekturcentret (Danish Architecture Centre)

Strandgade 27B, **T** 32571930, www.gammeldock.dk *Mon-Fri 1000-1700, Sat-Sun 1100-1600. Adults 30kr. Map 3, C10, p253*

This centre occupies an 18th-century warehouse on the site of the city's first dock and serves as an exhibition space for the work of designers and architects. The shows are usually first-rate and the warehouse building itself has been most sensitively restored. A stroll further north along Strandgade reveals more examples of smart renovation work on old warehouses that once stored huge quantities of skin and oil from whales caught off Greenland and Iceland, and brought here by boat in Denmark's colonial days.

Museums and galleries

- **Amalienborg** Royal apartments from 1863 to 1947 with original furniture, servant uniforms and table service, p65.
- **Arbejdermuseet** The Workers' Museum, culture and history of Copenhagen's working class, p84.
- **Arkitekturcentret** The Danish Architecture Centre, exhibitions, p96.
- **Bakkehusmuseet** Museum devoted to the arts of Denmark's Golden Age (1780-1850), p76.
- **Carlsberg Brewery Visitor Centre** Exhibition in the old brewery, with a drink of course, p75.
- **Christiansborg Slot** Royal receptions rooms, and access to the ruins of the first, 12th-century castle, p45.
- **Christiansborgs Slotskirke** A neo-classical church, restored to perfection, p52.
- **Dansk Design Centre** Semi-permanent and changing exhibitions of past and present Danish designs, p40.
- **Davids Samling** European, decorative and Islamic art, p71.
- **Den Hirschsprungske Samling** Danish art from the 19th century, p81.
- **Frederiksberg Slot** Monthly tours only of the castle now owned by the MOD, p78.
- **Frihedsmuseet** A museum devoted to the Danish resistance against Nazism, 1940-45, p66.
- **Geologisk Museum** Minerals, fossils and meteorites, from Denmark and Greenland, p84.
- **Københavns Bymuseum** City Museum, history of Copenhagen over the last 800 years, p73.
- **Kongelige Stalde Og Kareter** Royal Stables and Coaches, now a moderately interesting transport museum, p49.
- **Kunstindustrimuseet** Danish Museum of Decorative Art covering Europe, Japan and China, p63.

Museums and galleries

- **Marmorkirken** Marble Church, built from 1749 to 1894, guided tours and a tower to climb, p65.
- **Museum Erotica** The love life of Homo Sapiens, p62.
- **Nationalmuseet** Cultural history from the Stone Age onwards, mostly Danish but some Near East antiquities, p44.
- **National Photography Museum** A collection of snaps housed in the Black Diamond, p54.
- **Ny Carlsberg Glyptotek** Large collection of ancient art and exceptional French paintings and sculptures from the 19th and 20th centuries, p33.
- **Orlogsmuseet** Royal Danish Naval Museum, models and material of a maritime nature, p92.
- **Politihistorisk Museum** Police Museum, coshes and crimes of the city, p85.
- **Ripley's Believe it or Not Museum** Miniature world, p37.
- **Rosenborg Slot** Paintings, furniture, Crown Jewels, p68.
- **Royal Copenhagen Welcome Center** Porcelain factory of world-famous company, p76.
- **Statens Museum for Kunst** Danish National Gallery, collections of European art, p80.
- **Teatermuseet** Theatre Museum, housed in what was the Royal Court Theatre from 1767, p49.
- **Thorvaldsen's Museum** The sculptures of Bertel Thorvalden (1770-1844), large and super-large, p51.
- **Tøjhusmuseet** Royal Arsenal Museum, with vast collections of weapons, p49.
- **Tycho Brahe Planetarium** Space Theatre with IMAX films and exhibition, p74.
- **Vor Frelsers Kirke** Baroque church, over 300 years old, access to a twisting spiral staircase, p92.
- **Zoologisk Museum** Exhibits and models of animal life, p87.

North Zealand Coast, 101

Modish beach life on Bellevue or an aesthetic tan at the incomparable Louisiana gallery of modern art – two options close to the capital. Or, only 40 km north, Hamlet's castle bids 'Welcome to Elsinor'.

Roskilde and Hillerød, 110

At the end of a fjord, Roskilde gave the Vikings access to the sea and their peace-loving descendants enough space for a spectacular music festival. At nearby Hillerød, the Hollywood-like Frederiksborg Slot is as real as 17th-century castles can get.

Ishøj and Amager, 100

The Øresund bridge link to Sweden is transforming what was a sleepy backwater to the south. Two cool beaches and a strange museum beckon to the curious traveller.

Malmø, 118

Visiting another city in another country is a half-hour train trip away, a piece of cake. Shops, restaurants, parks and the music of the Swedish language.

North Zealand Coast

Copenhagen is on the island of Zealand and the northern coast of the island stretches as far as the town of **Helsingør**, *1¼ hours away by train from Central Station. Train-window views of the flat countryside between Copenhagen and Helsingør are unexciting but the beaches and the variety of accessible museums and castles makes for a number of possible excursions.*

▸▸ *See Sleeping p135, Eating and drinking p161 and Map p256*

Sights

★ Louisiana

Gammel Strandvej, Humlebæk, **T** 49190791, www.louisiana.dk
Mon-Tue and Thu-Sun 1000-1700, Wed 1000-2200. Adults 68kr, children 20kr. Humlebæk is 30 km north of Copenhagen – easily reached in under an hour on frequent trains from Central Station. From the station walk to the left along leafy Gammel Strandvej. It is a 10-min signposted walk.

Louisiana, a museum of modern art, is a fairly unmissable gallery for anyone interested in art. Quite apart from the permanent collections, the temporary exhibitions are often highly prestigious ones and a 2002 showing of the works of Georgia O'Keeffe at Louisiana, for example, was the only one in Europe. This translates into a steady and sometimes relentless stream of visitors, and a summer weekend is not the best time for a quiet contemplation of Giacometti.

The museum has an enviable coastal location, looking across the Øresund to southern Sweden, well away from urban distractions

! First built as a 19th-century villa, Louisiana's name comes from the highly peculiar fact that the villa's owner was married three times to women who were all called Louise.

and able to spread itself across a green so that the gardens become home to a stunning display of modern sculptures by Alexander Calder, Henry Moore, Joan Miro and Max Ernst. Around the gardens, gleaming pure white, single-storey rooms are spread out in an overlapping and sometimes confusing pattern. Highlights in the collections include a treasure trove of Giacometti's bronzes, canvases by Picasso, Bacon and Rothko and a sparkling array of Pop Art from the 1960s with work by Liechtenstein, Warhol, Oldenburg and Rauschenberg. Some aspects of modern European art are better represented at Louisiana than in London or New York, and not just modern Danish artists like Carl-Henning Pedersen and Robert Mortensen. There are examples of work by the COBRA artists, named after the first letters of the cities COpenhagen, BRussels, Amsterdam, a politically-conscious group which formed in 1948 and existed for three years before disbanding. The Danish painter Asger Jørn was a founding member of COBRA, which went on to influence Situationism. Louisiana has two floors devoted to shopping (see p205) and there is also an excellent café, dispensing sandwiches, meals and drinks.

Bakken and Bellevue Beach

Dyrehavsbakken (Bakken), Dyrehavevej 62, Klampenborg, **T** 39637300, www.bakken.dk *22 Mar-Jun and 5 Aug-26 Aug, Mon-Fri 1400-2400, Sat 1300-2400, Sun 1200-2400. Jul 4-Aug 1200-2400. Free or 198kr for a day pass (35 rides). From Central Station it's a 20-min train ride to Klampenborg, from there it takes 10 mins to reach Bakken.*

Bakken **amusement park**, built for the working classes in the same sort of way that Tivoli was designed for the well-bred, has rides galore, amusement arcades with hundreds of gaming machines, beer halls and fast-food joints. All the fun of the fair is here – carousels, shooting galleries, a wooden roller coaster from

★ **Attractions around**

- Louisiana, p101
- Viking Ship Museum, p114
- Roskilde Domkirke, p111
- Frederiksborg Slot, p114
- Arken Museum for Moderne Kunst, p116

1932 – and visitors often find it more enjoyable and less expensive than a trip to Tivoli.

Leaving Klampenborg station and walking in the opposite direction accesses the most attractive beach on the outskirts of Copenhagen, **Bellevue**. Its clean and safe water and green space for picnics and games attracts packs of semi-nude city folk in the summer. If it's all too much, consider retreating to the calm expanse of **Dyrehaven** (Deer Park) behind Bakken, where walking trails wend their way through beech woods. The manor house building that is hard to miss is Eremitagen, built as a hunting lodge in the early 18th century but no more open to the public now then it was then. Deer wander freely in Dyrehaven, and it is a relaxing spot in which to picnic and recharge batteries before succumbing to the alluring lights of Bakken.

Charlottenlund Beach and Park and Danmarks Akvarium

Kavalergården 1, Charlottenlund, **T** 39623283, www.danmarks@ akvarium.dk *Early Feb-late Oct 1000-1800, Jan-early Feb and late Oct-Dec 1000-1600. Adults 65kr, children 35kr. Buses 6, 166. S-Tog Charlottenlund.*

Just a little way south of Klampenborg, there is another small beach at **Charlottenlund**, and though not as pretty as Bellevue it becomes equally packed on a warm day. A more likely reason for being in Charlottenlund, a residential area for very well-heeled

An eventful life

Born in 1885 into a prosperous Danish family, the young Karen Blixen suffered the ordeal of her father's suicide when she was only 10. In her twenties, her life suffered another setback after an affair with her second cousin ended in tears but she bounced back with a loveless marriage to Baron Bror Blixen, the twin brother of the cousin. The baron owned a coffee farm in what is now Kenya and they lived there for years until marital rot set in and Karen ended up with syphilis from her philandering husband.

Divorced in 1925, she stayed in Africa and found solace with an Englishman, Denys Finch Hatton, until he died in a plane accident. She returned to her family home in Rungsted and took up writing. It was only after the success of *Seven Gothic Tales*, published in New York, that her fame began to impress Danish readers. More short stories and novels followed, and ones still in print include *Out of Africa*, *Seven Gothic Tales*, *Last Tales* and *On Modern Marriage and other Observations*.

Copenhageners, is the wonderful **Danmarks Akvarium**. One of Europe's largest aquaria, it is awash with fish, turtles, corals and crocodiles, and you don't need to be a child to feel enraptured by the eye-dazzlingly colourful collection of tropical fish. During school holiday periods and at weekends there are 'touch pools' for children, and the fish feeding time is 1400 on Wednesday, Saturday and Sunday (daily during school holidays).

Between the aquarium and Charlottenlund railway station, less than 20 minutes from Central Station, lies **Charlottenlund Park**, a happy hunting ground for picnickers. The park was the grounds of a 1690 royal residence and although the palace building from 1730 still stands it is privately owned and not open to the public. Around the palace there are walking trails and quiet spots to rest.

Ordrupgaard

Vilvordevej 110, Charlottenlund, **T** 39641183,
www.ordrupgaard.dk *Tue-Sun 1300-1700. Adults 35kr. S-Tog train to
Klampenborg and bus no 388.*

The **art museum** at Ordrupgaard, lying in a park of its own close
to Charlottenlund Park, has a small but select collection of French
and Danish art from the 19th and early 20th centuries. The Danish
paintings are not as interesting as those to be found hanging in
Den Hirschsprungske Samling but Ordrupgaard excels in French
works by Manet, Monet, Renoir, Ingres, Pissarro, Degas, Gauguin,
Matisse and Cézanne. The enchanting house, built in 1907, was the
home of the wealthy Wihelm Hansen who built up the collection
and bequeathed everything to the state.

Karen Blixen Museet

Rungsted Strandvej, Rungsted, **T** 45571057. *May-Sep Tue-Sun
1000-1700, Oct-Apr Wed-Fri 1300-1600, Sat-Sun 1100-1600. Adults
35kr. Trains to Rungsted depart from Copenhagen regularly and take
30 mins. From Rungsted station it is a 15-min walk or bus 388.*

Unless you have read or are planning to read some of Blixen's
stories, or remember the 1985 film of the book *Out of Africa*
starring Meryl Streep and Robert Redford, a visit to the house may
prove a little insubstantial. The rooms are furnished as they were
when she died here in 1962, hence the typewriter, the library of
books and the favourite chair of Denys Finch Hatton. There are
exhibits relating to her life in Africa and examples of her paintings
and drawings. The grounds of her house, where she is buried, are
large enough for a pleasant stroll and besides the centuries-old
beech trees there is an area set apart as a bird sanctuary, as Karen
Blixen wished. There is a café with an outdoor terrace and the shop
has the books, recordings, videos and posters relating to the writer.

I do not know if you remember the tale of the girl who saves the ship under mutiny by sitting on the powder barrel with her lighted torch…and all the time knowing that it is empty? This has seemed to me a charming image of the women of my time. There they were, keeping the world in order…by sitting on the mystery of the life, and knowing themselves that there was no mystery.

Isak Dinesen (1885-1962) also known as
Karen Blixen

Experimentarium (Danish Science Centre)

Tuborg Havnevej, Hellerup, **T** 39273333, www.experimentarium.dk
*May-mid-Sep, Tue-Sat 1000-1600, Sun 1000-1700. Mid-Sep-Apr,
Tue-Sat 1100-1500, Sun 1100-1600. Adults 89kr, children 62kr. Free
Wed. Buses 6, 21, 650S. S-Tog Hellerup and a 10-min walk.*

Roald Dahl would have loved the idea of turning a beer bottle
factory into a children's adventure playground, and this is more
or less what happened when the Experimentarium, the Danish
Science Centre, opened in an old Tuborg plant just 6 km north of
the city centre of **Hellerup**. The place can be overrun with school
parties, mostly morning visits, and weekends are busy times but
the well-deserved popularity of Experimentarium makes a visit
worthwhile, even without children. The world of nature, technology,
health and the environment is explored though hundreds of
hands-on experiments in a variety of simulated settings like the
moon's surface, the Hall of Mirrors, Mathematics, Moving Images.

Frilandsmuseet (Frilands Museum)

Kongevejen 100, Lyngby, **T** 33134411, www.natmus.dk *Apr-Sep,
Tue-Sun 1000-1700, Oct Tue-Sun 1000-1600. Adults 40kr. Free Wed.
Bus 184 from city centre, S-Tog to Sorgenfri and a 10-min walk.*

Using nearly 90 acres of land for the display of farmsteads and rural
cottages, Denmark's largest open-air museum makes for a grand
day out as there is lots to see and the surrounding parklands are
ideal for a picnic lunch. More than 100 listed buildings, from the
17th century onwards, provide tangible evidence of how people
lived their daily lives in rural Denmark, southern Sweden and parts
of northern Germany. Avoiding kitsch, the museum invites visitors
to wander at will, and having the English version of the site plan is
essential because the houses and buildings are not signposted as
such. Farm animals graze about the place and in summer there is a
schedule of demonstrations of folk arts.

Helsingør

www.visithelsingor.dk *Trains every 15-20 mins from Central Station or Nørreport S-Tog station. It's a 10-min walk to Kronborg.*

What wry comment would Hamlet make if he could see today's steady flow of visitors to his castle at Helsingør (Elsinor)? Would he be content with an ironical 'Welcome to Elsinor'? The famous castle of Hamlet, Kronborg, seen when you step out of Helsingør's railway station after a leisurely 45-km journey by train from Central Station, is where most visitors head for, but the town itself has its own appeal. Helsingør had prosperity thrust upon it when a royal toll was imposed in 1425 on every ship passing through the **Sound** at this, its narrowest, point and the town's history springs into a new life from that moment on. Nowadays, the toll having ceased in 1857, money is collected from willing Swedes who pilgrimage over on the ferry from Helsingborg for bulk purchases of beers and spirits. Whenever the ferry docks you'll see foot passengers heading in a beeline for the waiting off-licences, wheeling beer crates. Not only is the price of alcohol dearer in Sweden but it is also far more convenient to purchase in Denmark, as in Sweden it is only sold in special stores where proof of identity is required. With a copy of the useful map dispensed by the tourist office it is easy to find pedestrianized **Stengade**, the main shopping street, wander around the narrow alleyways that make up the medieval quarter of the town and rest in the market square, **Axeltorv**, for a drink. From Axeltorv, it is less than a five-minute walk to the town museum, or head back to near the tourist office where a venerable old ice cream parlour still enjoys a roaring trade on warm days.

Full of sound and fury signifying not much

The building of Kronborg was a massive undertaking and its fame as the most heavily defended of fortresses would have reached Shakespeare's London. When it came to the test, though, the castle was found wanting and its threatening presence on the coast proved ineffective in Denmark's war with Sweden over independ- ence in 1658. Nor could Kronborg stop Dutch and English fleets passing through the Sound in 1801. Seven years later, a special large oven was installed in the castle to make red-hot cannon balls in an attempt to improve its fire power, but it was too little and too late. The rest is silence.

Kronborg

Helsingør, **T** 49213078, www.kronborg.dk *May-Sep 1030-1700, Apr and Oct 1100-1600, Nov-Mar 1100-1500. Closed Mon between Jan-Apr and Oct-early Dec. Adults 60kr, children 25kr (the Copenhagen card only covers entry to the maritime museum section). See Helsingør, above, for transport information.*

Hamlet's castle first saw the light of day as a coastal fortification built in the 15th century by Erik of Pomerania (there could have been a famous tragedy by Shakespeare called *Erik*), the reigning king of Denmark, Norway and Sweden, to secure the control of the Øresund, the narrow strip of water between Denmark and Sweden and accessing the Baltic. A castle came soon after and Frederik II commissioned large-scale renovation work around 1600 only to have it all burn down some 30 years later. Rebuilt by Christian IV, but later plundered by the Swedes, the castle lapsed into a quiet existence and served as army barracks until the 1920s when the army moved out.

The Shakespearean atmosphere is all to be garnered on the outside, passing the moats and the oppressively heavy walls and stepping into a large cobbled, Renaissance-style courtyard that is wonderfully theatrical; not surprisingly, productions of *Hamlet* have been staged here. The castle interior is disappointing, relieved a little by some of the otherwise bare walls displaying information panels on Kronborg and the Shakespeare connection. The castle chapel falls short of any echoes of Hamlet or Ophelia that might be hoped for, and the maritime museum section of the castle can only muster a fairly sad collection of tired artefacts.

● *View the castle exterior and see the courtyard, but consider skipping the interior and blow the money instead on a bottle of wine and a picnic on the castle green.*

Roskilde and Hillerød

*There are two towns inland from Copenhagen that are well worth considering as day trips from the capital, **Roskilde** and **Hillerød**. There are two good reasons for visiting Roskilde – three if the festival is counted – an impressive **cathedral** and a terrific **Viking Ship Museum**, and it is only half-an-hour away from Copenhagen. Hillerød, again only a half an hour journey away, has the draw of the fairy tale red-brick palace of **Federiksborg Slot**.*

▸▸ *See Sleeping p136, Eating and drinking p162, Festivals and events p187 and Map p256*

About 5 trains an hour between Central Station and Roskilde taking half an hour. Bus no 600S from Hillerød.

◉ Sights

Roskilde Domkirke
Domkirkeplasden, Roskilde, **T** 46352700,
www.roskildedomkirke.dk *Apr-Sep, Mon-Sat 0900-1645, Sun
1230-1645; Oct-Mar, Tue-Sat 1000-1545, Sun 1230-1545. Adults 15kr,
children 10kr. Guided tours in English between 22 Jun and 18 Aug,
Mon-Fri, 1100, 1400, Sat 1100, Sun 1400. Adults 35kr, including
entrance fee, children 20kr. Train to Roskilde and a 10-min walk.*

For more than 1,000 years there has been a church on this site,
the present cathedral being started by Bishop Absalon, the
founder of Copenhagen, in the 1770s. Since then, though,
porches and chapels have been added on an almost ad hoc
basis and it is difficult to define the cathedral in terms of just
one architectural style. Roskilde had been the capital of Denmark
until the royals moved to Copenhagen in the early 15th century,
but its eccle- siastical importance remained undiminished and
it has remained the favourite burial place of Danish kings.
Nearly 40 in all are buried here and their richly decorated
sarcophagi are the main attraction of the church interior. While
some are modest enough, others are bombastic and silly, like
the Renaissance -style tomb of Christian IV set against a backdrop of paintings inside *trompe l'oeil* framing, including one of
the obese king posing as a militarist, and alongside a naff statue
of Christian by Thorvaldsen. The cathedral also has an amusing
clock that depicts St George slaying the dragon and making it
howl on the hour.

✕ Viking vessels
Around 1,000 years ago the Vikings sunk five of their ships in the fjord at Roskilde. They were excavated and form part of an engrossing exhibition at the Viking Museum.

★ Viking Ship Museum

Vindeboder 12, Roskilde, **T** 46300200, www.vinkingeskibsmuseet.dk
*May-Sep 0900-1700, Oct-Apr 1000-1600. Adults 60kr in summer, 45kr
in winter, children 35/28kr. Train to Roskilde and a 20-min walk or bus
216 or 605 from the station.* See also p236

Roskilde may be inland and some 30 km from Copenhagen but its
location at the southern tip of a fjord provides access to the sea;
enter the Vikings. Around 1,000 years ago they sunk five of their
vessels in the fjord, presumably a defensive measure aimed at
blocking an enemy attack by sea. The ships were excavated in 1962
and became the basis of a museum which now houses an
engrossing Vikings in Ireland exhibition and the five Viking ships
themselves. The exhibition of the ships, two trading vessels, two
warships and a smaller cargo vessel is supported by some 200
Viking artefacts found in Dublin, on loan from the National
Museum in Ireland, including well-preserved weapons, jewellery,
clothing and handicrafts. There is also an interesting Children's
Museum (see p220) and a good restaurant and shop.

The harbour outside the museum is home to four exact replicas
of Viking ships and work has started on a fifth, a 30-m warship
built in Dublin. The work takes place outdoors and visitors are
free to observe the building work in progress (the launch is
planned for 2004).

Frederiksborg Slot

Hillerød, **T** 48260439, www.frederiksborgmuseet.dk *Apr-Oct
1000-1700, Nov-Mar 1100-1500. Adults 50kr, children 10kr. Train to
Hillerød from Central Station.*

Only half an hour by train, a trip to the town of Hillerød and a
five-minute bus ride lands you outside Frederiksborg Slot, a
red-brick palace topped with copper spires that meets most
expectations of what a castle and royal residence should look like.

As royal pads go, you'll see a lot more for your money here than a trip to Buckingham Palace or Windsor and, while a booklet for 40kr explains everything, there are information sheets available in the chapel and some of the other rooms. In fact, there is so much to see that it's a matter of picking out your favourites, like maybe the ebony altarpiece and its silver ornamentation in the chapel where Denmark's monarchs were crowned between 1671 and 1840, the late 16th-century oak furniture in the Summer Parlour (room 22), the stupendous ceiling painting bordered by cherubic angels and bare-breasted women in room 30 or the breathtaking, reconstructed ceiling carved from wood in room 38 and the panels showing crafts and workmanship of the period. Every room has items of furniture that will catch your attention, like the bone-inlaid round chair in room 37 or the carved four-poster in room 35 that shows how much we have all grown over the last few centuries. Most of what is on show is not the original castle contents, but the result of JC Jacobsen deciding to fund restoration work and establish Det National-historiske Museum (National History Museum) within the rooms.

The museum shop sells jewellery, books and souvenirs. Hot drinks and ice creams are available and there is a Mexican restaurant across the road from the castle that opens at 1600. A picnic could be enjoyed in the surrounding landscaped gardens, with fine views of the ostentatious castle rising out of three islands in the middle of a lake, surrounded by its moat.

Ishøj and Amager

*In the wake of the Øresund bridge link to Sweden the area south of the city is being transformed and soon a complete new town, **Ørestad**, will be built west of the airport. At present there are two main destinations: **Ishøj** for its modern art gallery, and the small island of **Amager** for sandy beaches and rural relaxation. Both places are easily reached by train and bus from Copenhagen.*

▸▸ *See Sleeping p137 and Map p256*

◉ Sights

Arken Museum for Moderne Kunst
Skovvej 100, Ishøj, T43540222, www.arken.dk *Tue and Thu-Sun 1000-1700, Wed 1000-2100. Adults 65kr, children 35kr. Train to Ishøj, then a 25-min walk or bus 128.*

This is the most startling art gallery you will see on a visit to Copenhagen, due more to its appearance than the modernist art on display inside. Situated right by the seashore, Arken ('The Ark') forms the semblance of a ship in its architecture of glass, concrete and metal. Designed by Søren Robert Lund, the museum was built to celebrate Copenhagen's year as European City of Culture in 1996 and it still generates controversy. Critics say it distracts visitors from appreciating the work on display – and the interior is as dazzling and unusual as the exterior – but it is a museum of modern art and perhaps this makes the form of the building more understandable. The gallery's permanent collection is less interesting than the temporary exhibitions; check the web site to see what is on.

Amager
Buses 12, 13 to the beach, buses 30, 33, 36, 73E, 350S to Dragør.

Amager is a small island southeast of Copenhagen, easily reached by bus for access to its sandy beaches and delightful little village of **Dragør**. Until recently, Amager has remained in the shadow of cosmopolitan Copenhagen but the new metro line and the rapid development of the Ørestad area into a mini city is transforming the island. The main beach can be reached in less than 20 minutes

! The Øresund Bridge reconnects Denmark and Sweden, severed since the end of the Ice Age.

A morning in Malmö

A short train trip away, the Swedish city of Malmö offers more sights, shops, cobbled streets and squares.

by bus from the city centre and it's quite a contrast, physically and socially, with those along the North Zealand Coast (p101). The shallow water attracts families but, while there are some sandy places, there is no swathe of golden sand and the industrial landscape that forms the backdrop does not quite meet the needs of the beautiful young things who prefer the more socially exclusive beaches to the north. Amger's is Copenhagen's Coney Island, but with the benefit of two turquoise-coloured beach tavernas serving organic coffee, sandwiches and elderberry flower cordials.

Dragør is an idyllic-looking village, south of the beach, that has managed to preserve its identity as a modest farming and fishing community despite a steadily growing influx of city folk who are taking advantage of the new transport links. The **Dragør Museum**, situated near the harbour, tells the history of the village while the **Amager Museum**, situated in the village of Store Magleby which buses pass through en route to Dragør, focuses on the agricultural history of the area.

Malmö

Is it worth visiting Malmö? Probably not if your time is short, but given the ease of travel a day trip is a remarkably hassle-free way of seeing a part of Sweden, and current exchange rates (about 14 Swedish kroner (sek) to the pound sterling) mean dining and shopping costs less in Malmö than Copenhagen. Malmö also boasts a lively cultural festival in the third week of August.

▸▸ *See Sleeping p137, Eating and drinking p163 and Map p256*

◉ Sights

Trains glide over Øresund bridge, linking Copenhagen and Malmö in a comfortable 35-min journey. Ryanair *flights (p21) connect Malmö with London and there is a ferry link from Nyhavn. The tourist office,* **T** 341200, www.malmo.se, *is situated in the railway station. On sale is the Malmö Card (120sek for 1 day) which gives various discounts for places of interest, bike hire and train travel (unlikely to save you money unless your day is packed with activities). Also on sale are 100sek-tickets for guided sightseeing tours in English, while outside the railway station,* Rundan Canal Boats *depart on 45-min guided tours on the canals. The canal pedal boats for hire on Södra Promenade from mid-Apr to Aug for 100sek an hour are good fun.*

Malmö, the third largest city in Sweden, has a compact city centre and it is very easy for travellers to find their way about. The city has lovely large parks with miles of cycle tracks, and bikes can be hired. For a taste of the city, head for the main square, **Stor Torget**, a three-minute walk straight up from the station. Surrounding the central statue – of the king under whose rule Sweden was freed from Danish rule – are some plush hotels and the town hall, fashioned in the neoclassical style in the mid-19th century. Adjoining the main square is **Lilla Torg**, a charming cobbled square free of traffic and ebulliently full of café life and good restaurants (p163). In the immediate vicinity of Lilla Torg are the more interesting designer shops (p205) and a pedestrianized shopping street that leads to Triangeln, a triangular junction with a modern shopping centre.

Malmö's museums, *daily from 1000 to 1600*, are conveniently clustered in and around **Malmöhus Castle**, which is easily reached by bike or on foot. The castle, rebuilt by the Danish overlords in the 16th century, is now home to not-desperately-exciting exhibits of natural and cultural history, though up the road a short way the **Science Museum** has a more engaging collection of machines and technological wonders. Little information is provided in English but exhibits like the 1943 coastal submarine, which you can clamber aboard and poke around in, speak for themselves. **Malmö Konsthall**, *1100 to 1700*, the city's art gallery, is at St Johannesgatan, a short walk from Triangeln, and well worth a visit when an exhibition is on show.

Malmö's surprise is a sandy, one-mile-long **beach**, walkable from the railway station in under fifteen minutes. Safe for swimming, the highlight is the Kallbadhuset bathing house that retains its late-19th-century character and offers saunas and massages.

Sleeping

Accommodation costs much the same as in most capital cities in western Europe, with the best deals to be found on the internet at short notice. While the price categories used in this guide reflect rack rates for a double room in high season, they do not take account of special offers and weekend rates that are often available on the web. Reductions from 1540kr to 950kr for a double or from 2150kr to 1250kr for the pricier establishments are not unusual and hotels regularly reduce their rack rates to suit the market. When a large convention takes place in Copenhagen, special offers go out the window, but at other times top-notch hotels are worth considering. Accommodation can be booked through the Wonderful Copenhagen tourist office – www.bookcopenhagen.dk – in person or through the net, and there is a hotel booking service available at the airport tourist office. Another site worth looking at for useful information on less expensive accommodation is www.usit.dk Apartments are also available for rent by the day or by the week.

K Sleeping codes

LL	1900kr and over	**C**	900-1200kr
L	1700-1900kr	**D**	700-900kr
AL	1500-1700kr	**E**	500-700kr
A	1350-1500kr	**F**	300-500kr
B	1200-1350kr	**G**	300kr and under

Prices are for a double room in high season

Price

The main middle-of-the-road hotel area is behind Central Station, listed below under Vesterbro and Frederiksberg, where smart and comfortable double rooms can be found for below 1000kr. Classy hotels tend to be on the west side of the city, near Nyhavn and Kongens Nytorv, though they can also be found close to Central Station. Some hotels here also have rooms with shared bathroom facilities for around 650kr. Many hotels have free access to online computers though hostels and budget hotels tend to charge. A check-in time after 1400 is common, check-out time is usually 1100 at the latest.

Rådhuspladsen and around

Hotels

LL Palace, Rådhuspladsen 57, **T** 33144050, **F** 33145279, www.palace-hotel.dk *Map 3, C5, p252* Illustrious, tower-capped hotel that dates back to 1910 and overlooks the main square. Popular with Americans, the large bedrooms have dark wood furniture, most have baths, and there is a comfortable bar as well as a restaurant serving a good-value evening set meal. The best rooms have balcony windows overlooking the square.

AL Kong Frederik, Voldgade 25, **T** 33125902, **F** 33935901, www.remmen.dk *Map 3, C4, p252* If you like your hotels to look more posh than fashionable, this one fits the bill. Wood panelling, fireplace, portraits of the royal Frederiks hanging about, deep armchairs and antiques cluttering the public rooms; cosy in a heavy kind of way. Service around the clock and good restaurant.

A Alexandra, HC Andersens Boulevard 8, **T** 33744444, **F** 33744488, www.hotel-alexandra.dk *Map 3, C4, p252* Each bedroom in this very design-conscious, well-run hotel has a piece of classic Danish furniture and an original Danish painting (plus a foot bath tucked away in the wardrobe), with ultra-smart Christanborg fittings in the bathrooms. The non-smoking breakfast room, which is part of a smart restaurant (p143) serves health-conscious food, there is a bar and a sitting room with free internet, and bikes are freely available to guests.

B Ascot, Studiestræde 61, **T** 33126000, **F** 33146040, www.ascothotel.dk *Map 3, C3, p252* Tucked away in a side street, easily walkable from the railway station, the Ascot incorporates a 19th-century bath house and makes the best use of this in the attractive lobby. Smartly furnished bedrooms (with baths of course), free internet, a cosy bar, no restaurant, conservative atmosphere. Business travellers like this hotel.

C Danmark, Vester Voldgade 89, **T** 33114806, **F** 33143630, www.hotel-danmark.dk *Map 3, D6, p252* With Rådhuspladsen on the doorstep and Strøget a short walk away, the 53-room Danmark has an inner city feel, but not at the expense of peace and quiet. Modern-style bedrooms, with the better ones costing 200kr more a night.

Slotsholmen and around

Hotel

AL Mermaid, Løngangstræde 27, **T** 33126570, **F** 33152899, www.komfort-hotel.dk *Map 3, C5, p252* Unremarkable hotel but very well situated for city centre shopping and sightseeing and with a half-decent restaurant and an English-style pub next door. Nor is the Mermaid a noisy hotel even though tour groups periodically invade the reception area.

Apartments

LL-C Citilet Apartments, Fortunstræde 4, **T** 70222129, **F** 33913077, www.citilet.dk *Map 3, B7, p253* Quality one- and two-bedroomed apartments, bookable by the day or for a week (950kr for a day or 6,000kr week, 1,100kr for a day or 7,000kr for a week) offer a very worthy alternative to hotel accommodation. Fully furnished with kitchens and kitted out to a high standard.

Nyhavn and around

Hotels

LL D'Angleterre, Kongens Nytorv 34, **T** 33120095, **F** 33121118, www.remmen.dk *Map 3, A8, p253* If physical presence counts then this is Copenhagen's number one hotel, majestically dominating Kongens Nytorv and proudly proclaiming its five-star exclusivity. The inoffensive tone aspires more to luxury than snobbery, there is a pool and fitness centre, and the classical-style bedrooms and public areas are comfortably grand; afternoon tea (see p152) adds a touch of gentility to the establishment.

AL-C 71 Nyhavn, Nyhavn 71, **T** 33436200, **F** 33436201, www.71nyhavnhotelcopenhagen.dk *Map 3, B10, p253* Two warehouses, once storing Oriental spices and goods, have been converted into a smart, 150-room hotel on the corner of Nyhavn. The original beams lend a rustic touch to the luxury interior, including the bar and the above-average restaurant. Room rates, varying according to size and view, include breakfast, and drop in price at weekends; weekdays attract business groups.

A-B Hotel City, Peder Skramsgade 24, **T** 33130666, **F** 33130667, www.hotelcity.dk *Map 3, B9, p253* A typical Best Western hotel, with over 80 rooms ranging from standard to superior and above. Bedrooms are comfortable, predictably furnished in a modern style, and there is a café and breakfast room.

B-C Maritime, Peder Skramsgade 19, **T** 33134882, **F** 33150345, www.hotel-maritime.dk *Map 3, B9, p253* Next to the departure point for boats to Sweden, the Maritime has over 60 rooms, showers not baths, and some non-smoking rooms. Comfortable rather than homely. Worth checking the website for special offers that might be available.

C Sophie Amalie, Skt Annæ Plads 21, **T** 33133400, **F** 33117707, www.remmen.dk *Map 3, A10, p253* Large four-star hotel dating from mid-19th century located on the harbour front, the website has natty roving images of the different types of room that are available and those facing north look out to Amalienborg. Room rates do not include the breakfast buffet. Restaurant, sauna and a snug little bar.

D Hotel Bethel Sømandshjem, Nyhavn 22, **T** 33130370, **F** 33158570. *Map 3, B10, p253* An old seaman's hotel delightfully located in a characterful building at the end of Nyhavn. The cheapest rooms at 745kr are without a harbour view, while the

★ Designer digs

Best

- Radisson SAS Royal, p127
- DGI-byens, p129
- Alexandra, p124
- Cab Inn Scandinavia, p132
- 71 Nyhavn, p126

top rate of 895kr is for one of the spacious corner rooms with a grand view. A lift, showers not baths, a café for breakfast and snacks and Nyhavn nightlife down the street. A hotel with a history of serving travellers, and a sociable atmosphere to boot.

Vesterbro and Frederiksberg

Hotels

LL-L Radisson SAS Royal Hotel, Hammerichsgade 1, **T** 33426000, **F** 33426100, www.radissonas.com *Map 3, D3, p252* You wouldn't think so from the outside (p75) but the most stylish bedrooms in town are to be found here. Everything from the hotel building to the door knobs were originally designed by Arne Jacobsen (p42) and his style influenced the recent remodelling of the bedrooms by Yasmine Mahmoudieh. The bathrooms are striking in their use of glass mosaics and green granite floors, and each bedroom has the Swan chair, Jacobsen-designed floor lamp, plumbing details and door handles. Terrific restaurant too (p153), on the top floor.

LL-B First, Vesterbrogade 23, **T** 33788000, **F** 33788080, www.firsthotels.com *Map 3, D2, p252* Busy... with more than 400 rooms this is one of the largest and newest hotels in Denmark, allowing for the top three floors to be non-smoking and a set of 10 rooms specially designed for ladies (!), and all the overly compact bedrooms have an identical clean style of parquet flooring, cherry wood furniture and modern fittings. Breakfast is not included in the rack rates other than at weekends when room rates drop considerably in price. Beware of large coach groups periodically invading the hotel.

L Imperial, Vester Farimagsgade 9, **T** 33128000, **F** 33938031, www.imperialhotel.dk *Map 3, D3, p252* An unstuffy, four-star hotel that accommodates tour groups, business people and holidaymakers with equal efficiency, and the gregarious lobby bar reflects the mix of guests. As well as the standard bedrooms, there are 'Top Class' and 'Deluxe' rooms costing half as much again. Good restaurant (see p154). Well worth checking on the internet for a special rate.

L-AL Scandic Hotel Webers, Vesterbrogade 11B, **T** 33480400, **F** 33917700, www.scandic-hotels.com *Map 3, D3, p252* Part of a big chain of hotels across Scandinavia, and more than one in Copenhagen, the Scandic Hotel Webers has comfortable bedrooms, sauna, a bar with a happy hour of sorts, a relaxing atrium and above-average breakfasts. Easy to find, on the corner of Vesterbrogade and Colbjørnsnsgade, and not as noisy as the location might suggest.

A-B Grand, Vesterbrogade 9, **T** 33276900, **F** 33276901, www.grandhotelcopenhagen.dk *Map 3, D3, p252* A four-star hotel, popular with English travellers, with a cosy and friendly atmosphere and the marvellous Frascati restaurant (see p154) on the premises. Situated on the main road but not noisy from the inside; the rooms are not spacious and the lack of king-size beds deters Americans.

B Mayfair, Helgolandsgade 3, **T** 33314801, **F** 33239686, www.themayfairhotel.dk *Map 3, D3, p252* Near the corner of Vesterbrogade and Helgolandsgade, the hotel's superior rooms, unlike the regular, less expensive ones, have a bath. A bar on the premises but no restaurant; centrally located, though the decor is a little tired, perhaps.

B-E Absalon, Helgolandsgade 15, **T** 33242211, **F** 33243411, www.absalon-hotel.dk *Map 3, E3, p252* Less than five minutes from the station, a friendly and efficient hotel with free use of internet for guests and a range of room types to suit most budgets. The cheapest single/double/triple rooms at 495/650/850kr share washroom facilities while the main hotel block has smartly furnished doubles at 1100kr, but also singles and triples and, on the 5th floor, more expensive rooms with classy decor and extras. A popular hotel; advanced booking recommended.

B-D Nebo Mission, Istedgade 6, **T** 33211217, **F** 33234774, www.nebo.dk *Map 3, E3, p252* Clean, well-furnished two-star hotel with a pleasant breakfast room, no restaurant. Some of the bedrooms having a bath and others just a shower, and the least expensive rooms at 730kr share bathroom facilities.

C-D DGI-byens, Tietgensgade 65, **T** 33298050, **F** 33298059, www.dgibyen.dk *Map 3, E4, p252* If arriving by train, look for the hotel as the train draws into the station and take the rear exit from the station. Grey-coloured tone to the building, but not a grey aesthetic for what is one of the few city hotels that fulfils one's expectations of Scandinavian style and Danish modernism – dinky reception desk, design-conscious details, lines of Danish poetry on the bedroom walls, sleek, uncluttered, un-naff. Superb swimming pool and sports facilities (see p210) adjoin the hotel.

★ **Characterful**

Best
- D'Angleterre, p125
- 71 Nyhavn, p126
- Hotel Bethel Sømandshjem, p126
- Accommodation Løven, p132
- Hotel Skt Jørgen, p134

Sleeping

C Savoy, Vesterbrogade 34, **T** 33267500, **F** 33267501, www.savoy hotel.dk *Map 3, E1, p252* Over 60 rooms, from singles to family rooms sleeping four, some with showers and some with baths. Tea- and coffee-making facility in the rooms, cable television, a courtyard terrace, and a restaurant (closed on Mon). If you can get a reduction off the rack rates, the Savoy is not bad value as the place has a touch of character.

C-E Selandia, Helgolandsgade 12, **T** 33314610, **F** 33314609, www.hotel-selandia.dk *Map 3, E3, p252* Under the same management as the Absalon but a quieter building, dating from the late 1920s, and a less bustling atmosphere around check-out times. The light and airy breakfast room (note the clever trick painting on the wall) also has a calmer mood and the bedrooms tend to be better than Absalon's standard ones. All the bedrooms, whether sharing bathroom facilities or not, have television and trouser press.

C Top Hotel Hebron, Helgolandsgade 4, **T** 33316906, **F** 33319067, www.hebron.dk *Closed over Christmas. Map 3, E3, p252* The decorative features that distinguish the *Hebron* mostly date back to its opening over a century ago though there are some modern touches like the zappy lighting system over the stairs and the hotel is in good nick throughout. The superior rooms, 1040kr as opposed to 950kr for the standard doubles, are large and have baths.

D Centrum, Helgolandsgade 14, **T** 33313111, **F** 33233251, centrum.hotel@adr.dk *Map 3, E3, p252* The bedrooms, with tiny televisions, steel-framed beds, and showers, have a mix of faded furniture alongside some more modern pieces. The 1970s leather sofa and armchairs in the lobby suggest the Centrum has seen better days, but the breakfast room is pleasant enough and prices are competitive.

D Ibis Crown, Vesterbrogade 41, **T** 33212166, **F** 33210066, crown@accorhotel.dk *Map 3, E3, p252* Sister hotel to the Ibis, part of the same *Ibis Accor* chain, with identical rooms and prices. Set back off Vesterbrogade so noise should not be a problem. Hardly brimming with character but okay for a short stay if you just want a place to sleep.

D Ibis Star, Colbjørnsnsgade 13, **T** 33221100, **F** 33212186, star@accorhotel.dk *Map 3, E3, p252* A brighter, more functional hotel than the nearby Nebo; the snazzier bedrooms have smart, modern furniture; and crisp, clean colours define the decor. Showers not baths in most rooms, a bar and restaurant, and early breakfast available from 0400 (though breakfast is not included in the standard room rate).

E Cab Inn Copenhagen, Danasvej 32, **T** 33210400, **F** 33217409, www.cabinn.com *Closed between Oct and Mar.* *Map 3, B1, p252* For budget hotel accommodation there is nothing to beat Copenhagen's two Cab Inns, though anyone prone to claustro-phobia might feel penned in by the extremely compact rooms. A design triumph in streamlining, each cabin – the ship term is very appropriate – packs in a shower room, toilet, television, tea-and coffee-making facility, and instructions on the wall on how to flip open the bed and tables. Singles, doubles, triples and four-bed cabins at 510/630/750/870kr and breakfast 50kr. Go for it – if you plan to spend as much time as possible outside of your hotel room.

E Cab Inn Scandinavia, Vodroffsvej 55, **T** 35361111, **F** 35361114, www.cabinn.com *Map 3, A1, p252* As above in every respect, though open all year, and sharing the same pleasant, quiet, residential neighbourhood. A non-touristy area but a bakery and pizzeria are close by, a bar on the nearby corner with Johnstrups Allé, and Cafésius (p156) not far away doing drinks and meals until late.

Hostels and guesthouses

E-G Accommodation Løven, Vesterbrogade 30, **T/F** 33796720, 33158646, www.loeven.dk *Map 3, E2, p252* Opposite the Ibis Crown hotel, the entrance to this centrally located guesthouse is easy to miss. The bedrooms are a little bare, no television, but clean and adequate. Doubles and singles with shower and toilet are 550-750kr/495-595kr, those sharing bathroom facilities are 400-500kr/350-400kr, and bedrooms for three to six people are 200-300kr. There is a bakery next door, and with free use of Løven's kitchen guests can save money on meals. The only problem is traffic noise from the street and the hideously loud ringing of nearby church bells in the morning.

G City Hostel, Absalonsgade 8, **T** 31312070, **F** 31235175. *Map 3, E1, p252* A summer-only hostel, opening between 5 May and 25 August, centrally located behind the City Museum on Vesterbrogade. Open 24 hours, the large dormitory is less comfortable than the smaller upstairs rooms. No private rooms. There is a kitchen, but breakfast is available for 25kr on top of the 130kr for a bed.

Around the Three Lakes

Hotels

A Kong Arthur, Nørre Søgade 11, **T** 33111212, **F** 33326130, www.kongarthur.dk *Map 4, G3, p254* The regal exterior, swanky lobby and richly carpeted foyer announce a quality hotel and four-star Kong Arthur, with its back to the city as it looks out across the lakes, strives to make the mark. Bedrooms – some non-smoking ones available – are classical in style with antique furniture adding grace. The Brøchner restaurant specializes in Danish-French cooking and the bar is open 24 hours. Worth a whirl when special offers charge two nights for the price of one.

B-C Ibsens, Vendersgade 23, **T** 33131913, **F** 33131916, www.ibsenshotel.dk *Map 4, H4, p254* A pleasant three-star, children-friendly hotel with over 100 bedrooms, decorated in a variety of slightly different styles but sharing an easy-going relaxed look. A restaurant and breakfast room, and a good location close to the lakes, lively Nørreport, bus routes and train station.

C Hotel Nora, Nørrebrogade 18B, **T** 35372021, **F** 35372621, www.hotelnora.dk *Map 4, G3, p254* A smart new hotel on busy Nørrebrogade with large bedrooms, showers not baths, complete with coffee- and tea-making facility and a fridge. Internet access. The rooms are tastefully furnished in a contemporary style, brightly decorated with framed modern art on the walls. Singles and four- and six-bed family rooms also available.

D Hotel Rye, Ryesgade 115, **T** 35265210, **F** 35265214. *Buses 1, 6, 14, or 650 from outside Central Station or the town hall. Map 4, B6, p254* A small hotel situated in a quiet location by one of the lakes and with a large park two minutes away. Reasonably priced rooms from 700/500kr for a double/single and three- and four-bedrooms for 900/1000kr. Showers and toilets are shared but every bedroom has kimonos and slippers, and home-made buns at breakfast time.

D-G Jørgensen, Rømersgade 11, **T** 33138186, **F** 33155105, www.hoteljorgensen.dk *Map 4, H4, p254* A good range of rooms for travellers on a budget, from doubles with a bathroom for 700kr, down to around 500kr for ones with a bathroom on the corridor and dorm rooms for 120kr. This is as good as you will get in Copenhagen for these prices and the breakfast buffet is not a skimpy one. The bedrooms are small, though, in this gay-friendly hotel.

E Hotel Skt Jørgen, Julius Thomsensgade 22, **T** 35371511, **F** 35371197, st.jorgen@teliamail.dk *Bus no 250S from the airport stops near by, as do nos 2, 11, 67 and 68. Look for a clothes store on the corner with an anchor sign, the hotel is next door. Map 4, H4, p254* In the same family for 40 years, this venerable old hotel has the distinction of bringing breakfast to your room (in the absence of a breakfast room) between 0700 and 1000. Two bathrooms on each floor, though each bedroom has a sink and mirror. Singles and larger bedrooms available for up to five people.

Hostels

G Sleep-In, Blegdamsvej 13A, **T** 35265059, **F** 35435058, www.sleep-in.dk *Open from late Jun to end of Aug. Reached by buses 1, 6 14, and 250S from the airport, or a 1-km walk from Østerport station. Map 4, B6, p254* This is a very large but friendly hostel with over 280 beds spread over a hall-like building, partitioned off into sections. A kitchen, free lockers, a café and internet access (not free). Sleep-In, at 90kr a night plus 30kr for blanket and sheet if without a sleeping bag, is pretty full most of the time, which makes it very busy.

F-G Sleep-In Heaven, Struenseegade 7, **T** 35354648, www.sleepinheaven.com *From outside Central Station on the Tivoli side , take bus no 8 with Tingbjerg on the front and ask to be put off at Griffenfeldtsgade, the fifth stop, by a 7-eleven on the corner. Map 4, G1, p254* A kitchen-less hostel, restricted to travellers aged 16-35, with large dormitories partitioned into smaller sections, and two doubles still sharing bathroom facilities, for 450kr per room. The dorm beds are 110kr per night and a one-off 30kr payment for a bed sheet. Open 24 hours, safety deposit boxes and internet access (not free), this is a bright and cheerful hostel. Breakfast is served, beer and wine is sold in the café, there is a backyard with picnic tables, and a pool table.

Around Copenhagen

Helsingør

A Marienlyst, Ndr Strandvej 2, **T** 49214000, **F** 42914900, www.marienlyst.dk *Bus no 340 from outside the railway station stops outside Marienlyst Station, or take a local train from Helsingør.* A hotel for pampering yourself with the help of an indoor swimming pool, sauna, and casino. A grand dining room sets the tone of relaxed indulgence. If you don't mind a hotel with a bourgeois tone, the Marienlyst is worth checking out on the internet for the various short-stay packages available.

G Helsingør Camping 'Grønnehave', Strandalleen 2, **T** 25311212, www.helsingorcamping.dk Well-equipped camping ground with a beach on the doorstep. Situated near the Marienlyst hotel and a short walk away from Kronborg. A conven- ience store, laundry facilities, tennis courts within walking distance. Chalets with their own bathrooms can also be hired, from 400kr.

Charlottenlund

G Charlottenlund Fort, Strandvejen 144B, **T** 39623688. Bus no 6 takes you straight through to Charlottenlund (p103) and stops next to this lovely campsite in the middle of the beach, 6 km from the city centre. Utilizing a disused, 19th-century fort, this smart camping ground has modern facilities, though no cabins or tents for hire.

Roskilde

B Prindsen, Algade 13, Roskilde, **T** 46309100, **F** 46309150, www.hotelprindsen.dk In the centre of town on a pedestrianized street, Prindsen is one of the oldest hotels in Denmark. While the regular rate for singles/doubles is 1095/ 1295kr, a stay becomes a more viable proposition when the discounted rate of 850/950kr is available, including breakfast.

G Roskilde Camping, Baunehøjvej 7, Veddelev, Roskilde, **T** 46757996, **F** 46754426, www.roskildecamping.dk *About 4 km from town, bus no 603 for Veddelev stops nearby*. A three-star camping ground with views of the fjord and the town. A shop, cabins for hire, and a sandy beach with a bathing jetty.

G Roskilde Vandrerhjem, Vindeboder, Roskilde, **T** 46352184, **F** 46326690, www.danhostel.dk/roskilde A hostel, next to the Viking Ship Museum, that with some of the 40 rooms looking out to the fjord can be a cool place for an overnight stay. Unless booked in with a pass card, the hostel only opens between 0800 and 1200 and 1600 to 2200. Always full at festival time, there are private rooms as well as dorm beds, kitchen and TV lounge.

Amager

G Danhostel Copenhagen Amager, Vejlandsallé 200,Amager, **T** 32522908, **F** 32522708, www.danhostel.dk/copenhagen *Take S-Tog to Sjælør and then bus no 100S, which stops outside, or bus no 46 from Central Station, or no 250S from the airport or from Central Station (bus stop on the right after exiting on the Tivoli side); a 20-min journey.* Huge HI hostel, over 500 beds and lots of private rooms, open 24 hours, with a kitchen but breakfast- buffet and dinner menus at reasonable prices. Good facilities, including launderette and internet.

Bellahøj

G Danhostel Copenhagen Bellahøj, Herbergvejen 8, Bellahøj. **T** 38289715, **F** 38890210, www.danhostel.dk/bellahoej *A 15-min bus journey using no 2 from Rådhuspladsen (Town Hall Square), or no 11 from Central Station, or night bus no 82N from Rådhuspladsen.* Situated in a quiet suburb some 5 km northwest of the city centre, an HI hostel with 250 beds, including family rooms, 24-hour reception, launderette, breakfast and evening meals available, plus kitchen.

Malmö

L Radisson SAS, Östergatan 10, **T** (040) 6984000, **F** 6984001, www.radissonsas.com Large bedrooms, with a choice of oriental, ecological or Scandinavian room style, and a good restaurant (see p163). The best time to stay is Friday to Sunday when the rate drops from 2240sek to 920sek.

C Comfort Hotel, Carlsgatan 10C, **T** (040) 6112511, **F** 6112310, www.choicehotels.se   Situated behind the railway station, this is a well-run hotel that deserves its name, with a kitchen that provides breakfast, hot drinks and cake throughout the day, and an evening buffet as part of the room rate. A double is 1095sek, dropping to 760sek on Friday and Saturday.

There is far more to eating in Copenhagen than the ubiquitous *smørrebrød* – petite piles of meat, fish and cheese on a slice of rye bread – and a rich variety of cafés and restaurants to choose from. Unpretentious pubs serve traditional, economically priced meals at lunchtime wherever *dagens ret* ('meal of the day') appears on a menu or blackboard. There are fast food shawarma, kebab and pizza joints offering plenty of alternatives to Mcimperialism. Cafés and bars merge into one kind of informal establishment serving drinks and food throughout the day, with pavement tables wherever the space allows and, apart from some of the self-consciously stylish places, offer good value-for-money snacks and light meals. Indian and Thai food is available and recent years have seen a blossoming of restaurants featuring modern Danish cuisine, usually mixing traditional Danish elements with Italian, French, Japanese and other influences. Vegetarians should have little difficulty finding suitable food, especially if fish is eaten, and vegetarian dishes (and sometimes vegetarian menus) feature in many restaurants.

K Eating codes

Price

KKK	350kr and over
KK	200-350kr
K	200kr and under

Prices refer to the cost of a three-course meal, excluding drinks

Gammel Strand has a cluster of upmarket fish restaurants and cafés with outdoor tables for Danes intent on displaying their superior lifestyle. Nyhavn offers a more democratic mood for wining and dining, while around Vesterbrogade there is a pleasing variety of places ranging from the Danish bakery (*konditorier*) and kebab-style eateries to specialist restaurants like the incomparable Passagens Spisehus (p154). Værnedamsvej, a street that runs off Vesterbrogade, has a number of non-touristy places to eat and is worth a browse. Nørrebro is rich hunting ground for cafés and bars offering good meals as opposed to a 'dining experience'. The cafés in the major art galleries and museums are nearly always stylish and worth a visit. The best of modern Danish cuisine is be found all over the city. For help in reading menus, see Language, p238.

Rådhuspladsen and around

Restaurants

KKK La Crevette, Vesterbrogade 3 (Tivoli), **T** 33146003. *19 Apr-22 Sep, 15 Nov-22 Dec 1200-2400. Map 3, D4, p252* Top-drawer fish restaurant in Tivoli (adjoining Brasserie N, see below), with red-aproned staff in bow ties and waistcoats providing a smart service at tables decorated with attractive flower arrangements on white tablecloths. The four-course set evening menu might start with lobster cappuccino before a main dish of bass with couscous and

Wine tasting

Many restaurants have a wine menu that chooses an appropriate kind of wine to accompany each of the food courses and, for a set price, you are served with a glass of each different wine as the meal progresses. An admirable introduction to the art of choosing the right wine for different types of food, every budding foodie should go for it at least once, and only the more parsimonious restaurants will deny diners a second glass of wine they particularly enjoy. On regular wine lists, the house wines are not labelled as such but they are usually the first on the list. See also box, p154

orange-Dijon sauce; consider spoiling yourself with the generous set wine menu at 305kr per person.

KKK Truffle Café & Restaurant, Vestergade 29-31, **T** 33131500. *Sun 1130-1500 Mon-Sat and 1130-2200. Map 3, C5, p252* Superb variety of food in a new, non-smoking restaurant, with sofa seats and chairs down the length of the stylish interior, and outdoor tables against a burnt-orange background. The 400kr-set meals for two in the café are almost half the price of those in the restaurant. Sushi with a Kirin in a tall glass is recommended; set wine menu adds 125kr to the bill.

KKK-K Taj Indian Restaurant, Jernbanagad 3-5, **T** 33131010. *1200-2330. Map 3, C3, p252* Silver chairs, statues of deities from the sub-continent, vast cluster of bangles hanging from the ceiling, not to mention Indian chefs, help make this a classic Indian restaurant (and the first in Denmark). Sixteen set menus from 195kr to a gargantuan feast at 595kr, no buffets, and old favourites like king prawns, chicken tikka and tandoori dishes.

KK Brasserie N, Vesterbrogade 3 (Tivoli), **T** 33146003, www.nimb.dk *19 Apr-22 Sep 1200-2300, 15 Nov-22 Dec 1200-1430. Map 3, D4, p252* Oriental glitz on the outside, busy Gallic brasserie inside, and an appealing international menu at night. Danish lunch with herrings or two or three choices from the *smørrebrød* menu will keep the bill below 150kr, while the evening set meal (with vegetarian option) for 315kr is good value compared to the à la carte choices.

KK-K L'education nationale, Larsbjørnstræde 12, **T** 33915360. *1200-1600, 1800-2230. Map 3, B5, p252* Red-chequered tablecloths, a glimpse of Jean-Luc Godard amongst the myriad of posters, blackboard menu in French and Danish and, on Thursday nights, a two-piece jazz band squeezed into a corner. French-style food, of course, and an affordable set meal makes L'education nationale a perennial favourite with Copenhageners.

KK Mühlhausen Brasserie, Alexandra, HC Andersens Boulevard 8, **T** 33744466. *1130-2400. Map 3, C4, p252* A café, bar and brasserie with an appreciative eye for Danish design – Kaare Klint church choir chairs, Borge Mogensen sofas and PH chandeliers, and check the fittings in the washrooms. Southern European cuisine, popular with discerning Danes.

KK Peder Oxe, Gråbrødretorv 11, **T** 33110077. *1130-0100. Map 3, B6, p252* Hard to classify the cuisine, classy international/ Danish/ French, but the wide-ranging menu is full of interesting ideas and the characterful interior makes Peder Oxe an ideal restaurant for an evening out, especially with a wine bar in the vaulted cellars of this very old building.

K Jensen's Bøfhus, Gråbrødretorv 15, **T** 33327800. *Mon-Thu, Sun 1100-2230, Fri-Sat 1100-2330. Map 3, B6, p252* Set in an appealing pedestrianized square of much character. Steaks,

Eating and drinking

★ Meal to remember

Best

- Passagens Spisehus, p154
- Skt Gertruds Kloster, p148
- Alberto K, p153
- Spiseloppen, p160
- La Crevette, p141

burgers and eat-all-you-can meals of barbecued ribs with chips and coleslaw are not half bad. Outdoor tables too, good for coffee and cakes anytime. Other Jensen's Bøfhus restaurants are in Kultorvet 15, and Vesterbrogade 11A.

K RizRaz, Store Kannikestræde 19,
T 33323345. *1130-2400. Map 3, B5, p252* The second and newer RizRaz restaurant, occupying a 19th-century university building, has the identical budget-priced buffets and reasonably-priced drinks as the original (see p146). Of the four seating areas (plus pavement tables), the one behind the bar is the most attractive if making your visit an evening out.

Cafés

K Aløj Dee Take Away, Fiolstræde 30, **T** 33328206. *Mon-Sat 1000-2100. Map 3, A5, p252* Pretty good Thai take-away food but with a couple of tables and stools inside and a few outside on the pavement as well. Fine for a quick bite and a reminder of Thai tastes; at the Nørreport station end of Fiolstræde.

K Café Glyptotek, Dantes Plads 7, **T** 33418141, www.glyptoteket.dk *Tue-Sun 1000-1600. Map 3, E5, p252* Overlooking the Winter Garden in the Ny Carlsberg Glyptotek (see p33), the atrium café serves enticing goodies which, in the cultured surroundings, somehow seem to taste more edifying than one has been led to expect of home-made cakes and fruit tarts.

K Café Paludan, Fiolstræde 10, **T** 33150675. *0800-2000. Map 3, B5, p252* Fiolstræde was, for a long time, a rag-bag of a street but this bookshop café is part of its reinvention as a hip cultural ghetto for would-be intellectuals. The obligatory jazz music in the background, and over 20 kinds of coffee to accompany a croissant or two while reading Kierkegaard.

K La Glace, Skoubogade 3, **T** 33144646. *Mon-Thu 0830-1730, Fri 0830-1800, Sat 0900-1700. Map 3, B5, p252* Agreeably old-fashioned pâtisserie, dating back to the 1870s, right down to the marble-top tables, and matronly waitresses serving hot chocolate, and cakes (from 21kr) with cream so pure and soft you'd think there must be a cow or two at the back of the shop. The inside can feel a bit stuffy sometimes and there is one outdoor table on the pedestrianized street.

Slotsholmen and around

Restaurants

KKK Krogs Fiskerestaurant, Gammel Strand 38, **T** 33158915. *Mon-Sat 1130-1600, 1730-2400. Map 3, C6, p252* Outdoor tables on the cobbled pavement under one large umbrella and a bourgeois interior of oval mirrors, green walls and carpets, and seascape paintings. Lunch won't leave much change out of 300kr and the richly-laden dinner menu – lobster, oysters, caviar, organic salmon with scallops, sole with lobster and truffles – is priced accordingly.

! Jacobsen's cutlery was futuristic enough to be used in Kubrick's 2001: A Space Odyssey.

KK Gammel Strand, Gammel Strand 42, **T** 33912121. *Mon-Sat 1200-1500, 1730-2200. Map 3, C6, p252* Fish dishes served at outdoor tables with fine linen, or in more formal indoors setting. Two-course fish menu at lunchtime stays below 200kr per person, with less expensive dishes like a lunch plate, herring plate, or caesar salad. Evening set meal is around 300kr.

KK Søren K, Søren Kierkegaards Plads 1, **T** 33474949. *1100-2230. Map 3, D8, p253* On the ground floor of the Black Diamond (see p146). Set meals and the vegetarian menu keep prices within the mid-range bracket (if you can resist the set wine menu) and, with menus changing every few months, this is a terrific place to enjoy creative cooking like pike with lobster-filled gnocchi or chocolate mousse with parsley. Lunch dishes between 65kr and 175kr.

KK Spisehuset/La Bella Notte, Magstræde 14, **T** 33326173/ 33145270. *Tue-Thu 1800-2130, Fri-Sat 1800-2200. Map 3, C6, p252* Funky in a Danish kind of way with sofas and chairs on bare floor boards and deep red walls with assorted oil paintings. In summer (Spisehuset tends to close in July), the *La Bella Notte* restaurant also opens downstairs in an alleyway with washing lines overhead to create instant Italia. A tasty house salad, but anything from tacos to Thai can pop up; all at healthy prices, coming in at the bottom end of the mid-range bracket.

● *Make a night of it at* Spisehuset/La Bella Notte, *sipping pre-dinner cocktails at the theatre bar downstairs and dropping in later around the corner at* Galathea Kroen, *see p147, to enjoy good jazz and laid-back company.*

K RizRaz, Kompagnistræde 20, **T** 33150575. *1130-2300. Map 3, C6, p252* The prices for the buffets, 49kr for lunch (until 1600) and 59kr for dinner, act like a magnet for hungry vegetarians. A super choice that includes falafel, pitta bread, aubergine, feta cheese, tahina and lots more. Wine is 25kr a glass, 150kr a bottle, so it's a quick bite before heading off into the night, or take it slow for a budget boozy night out.

Cafés

KK-K Akvavit, Gammel Strand 44, **T** 33328844. *Mon-Sat 1000-2400, Sun 1000-2200. Map 3, C6, p252* More of a lifestyle café than a place for a hearty meal, *Akvavit's* outdoor tables are usually full with beautiful people resting in the shade of broad umbrellas while gazing out at Christiansborg, and the pedestrians milling past. A good range of drinks, *smørrebrød* averaging 100kr each, salads and bagel sandwiches.

K Galathea Kroen, Rådhusstræde 9, **T** 33116627. *Mon-Thu 1800-0200, Fri-Sat 1800-0500. Map 3, C6, p252* A crowd of regulars testify to the satisfying mix of quality jazz and an Indonesian ristaffel of eat-all-you-want curry, as well as steaks, cigars and malt whiskies. Lots of character and enough artefacts hanging about the place to make you think you've stumbled into an ethnographic museum.

K Kanal Caféen, Frederiksholms Kanal 18, **T** 33115770. *Mon-Fri 1130-1900. Map 3, D6, p252* Low-beamed, cosy interior and canalside tables outside looking across to Slotsholmen. Home-made pâté, curried herrings or poached and pickled with smoked

Eating and drinking

eel, roast pork and pickles, gorgonzola with egg yolk, chicken and mayonnaise salad – mostly in the 40-60kr range.

K Øieblikket, Søren Kierkegaards Plads 1, **T** 33474747. *Mon-Fri 1000-1900, Sat 1000-1400. Map 3, D8, p253* On your right after entering the lobby of the Royal Library, this café is named after the publication that brought Kierkegaard into print and complements the *Søren K* restaurant (see p146). A fine spot for a light sandwich or quiche repast after visiting Christiansborg.

K Slotskælderen hos Gitte Kik, Fortunstræde 4, **T** 33111537. *Mon-Fri 1100-1500. Map 3, B7, p253* A stone's throw from the Folketinget (Danish Parliament, p48), where you could spot Danish MPs if any of them were that famous, this is a good spot for its choice of *smørrebrød*.

Nyhavn and around

Restaurants

KKK Le Sommelier, Bredgade 63-5, **T** 33114515, www.lesommelier.dk   *Mon-Fri 1200-1400, Mon-Sun 1800-2200. Map 4, G10, p255* French-style cuisine offers fine dining and top-drawer wines in a relaxed setting. Come in the evening for fewer suits and a more varied set of customers. Menu in French and Danish with dishes – cochon de lait, fèves et piment, pomme purée a l'huile vierge, sauce a l'estragon – verging on the adventurous. Lurking in the wings as a Michelin contender?

KKK Skt Gertruds Kloster, Hauser Plads 32, **T** 33146630, www.sgk.as *1600-0200. Map 3, A6, p252* A medieval monastery setting and a dining experience. Pre-dinner drinks served in a library setting before diners move to one of the candle-lit dining

★ Arty places for lunch

Best

- Café Glyptotek, p144
- Courtyard of Kunstindustrimuseet, p63
- Nationalmuseet, p44
- Statens Museum for Kunst, p80
- Café Lars Nørgård, p157

areas where modern Danish cuisine is served. The wine cellar can be visited, and a wine menu is an option with meals. Menu from 425-690kr.

KKK-KK L'Alsace, Ny Østergade 9, **T** 33145743, www.alsace.dk *Mon-Sat 1130-2400. Map 3, B8, p253* Set meals and daily specials that approach the exquisite. Spoil yourself with the salade gourmandise (shrimps, lobster and foie gras), and the rhubarb gateau is a firm favourite after one of the fish courses. Always a vegetarian main course, set meals from under 350kr to nearly 500kr. Menu in French and Danish.

KKK Cap Horn, Nyhavn 21, **T** 33128504. *1130-2300. Map 3, A9, p252* Consistently good *smørrebrød* and authentic herring table. Lively night-time atmosphere when an outdoor table often requires a reservation. The food is modern Danish with a continental inflexion, bare floorboards and a comfortable bar area. Bizarre menu arrangement that starts with the desserts.

KKK Egoisten, Hovedvagtsgade 2, **T** 33127971. *Mon-Sat 1200-1500, 1800-2300. Map 3, A8, p252* If Nyhavn is too clamorous for your liking, consider retreating to the other side of Kongens Nytorv and checking out the food scene in Egoisten. New owners are changing everything and the prospects look good, with the menu still in the process of inventing itself. Expect oysters and lemon or

Perfect pastries
In Denmark, Danish pastries are called Wienerbrod (Viennese Bread) after an influx of Austrian bakers when Danish bakers went on strike.

herrings and potato salad for lunch and, at night, attractively presented fish and meat dishes at reasonable prices.

KKK Sult, Vognmagergade 8, **T** 33743417. *Tue-Sat 1800-2400. Map 3, A7, p253* Inside the Danish Film Institute and named after the novel by Knut Hamsun (Sult means 'hunger'), the name also plays on the word Sult ('End') which appears at the end of Danish films. New-York style restaurant creating Mediterranean dishes with panache, like slow-baked tomatoes with smoked mozzarella, lamb with figs and cumin on couscous.

KKK Zeleste, Store Strandstræde 6, **T** 33160606. *1100-2230.*
Map 3, A9, p253 For quality cuisine Zeleste more than matches the
trendy restaurants on Nyhavn, and for atmosphere book one of the
courtyard tables. The main draw is the fish, with terrific starters of
lobster or steamed mussels, competing with the asparagus and
truffles, and the popular Sunday brunch needs a reservation. Voted
in 2002 as having the most romantic courtyard restaurant in the city.

● *Enjoy the best of both worlds with excellent food at* Zeleste *and
a pre- or after-dinner drink around the corner on Nyhavn at* Nyhavn
17 *(live music after 2100).*

KK-KKK Els, Store Strandstræde 3, **T** 33141341. *Mon-Sat
1200-1500, 1730-2200, Sun 1730-2200. Map 3, A9, p253* The murals
of this classy-looking and cosy restaurant date back to the 19th
century when the building was an elegant coffee house patronized
by theatre folk from the nearby Royal Theatre. Set three- and
four-course meals keep prices within the mid-range bracket but à la
carte spiced lamb or duck push into the expensive category.

Cafés

K-KK Café Anton, Illum Department Store, Østergade 52,
T 33144002. *Mon-Thu 1000-1830, Fri 1000-1930, Sat 0900-1430.
Map 3, B7, p253* Pizzas, salads and steaks on the fourth floor, with
natural light pouring in from the glass roof, and a narrow terrace
where *smørrebrød* can be enjoyed for around 30kr.

KK-K Café Petersborg, Bredgade 76, **T** 33125016. *Mon-Fri
1145-1500, 1700-2030. Map 4, G10, p255* What Danes call a
hygee restaurant – low-ceiling, exposed beams, wood panelling –
undeniably cosy and difficult to leave once settled around a table
and stuck into the Danish-language menu. *Smørrebrød* lunch,
around 45kr an item, while main courses tend to be meat-based

★ **Vegetarian**

Best

- Taj Indian Restaurant, p142
- RizRaz restaurants, p144 and p146
- Morgenstedet, p161
- Govindas, p157
- Søren K, p146

and are in the 75-160kr bracket. Look, too, for the half-dozen or so specials.

K Café Sommersko, Kronprinsensgade 6, **T** 33148189. *Mon-Thu 0800-2400, Fri 0800-0200, Sat 0900-0200, Sun 1000-2400. Map 3, B6, p252* This café has been around for ages and although spacious you can still be kept waiting for a table. Useful for a break from exhausting shopping on Købmagerade, with a vegetarian or meat brunch being the house specialty, from 84kr, and always good for a coffee break with tempting cakes and pastries. At night the place becomes more hip, competing with the Zoo Bar opposite (see below).

K Mojo, Gothersgade 26, **T** 33320105. *Mon-Thu 0800-2200, Sat 0930-2300, Sun 1030-2000. Map 3, A8, p253* Open, Swedish-American style, surrounded by glass, with the *de rigueur* range of coffees, and sandwiches served with a choice of sauces for dipping into. On the corner of Gothersgade and Borgergade, the service at Mojo is refreshingly brisk and efficient.

K D'Angleterre, Kongens Nytorv 34, **T** 33120095. *1500-1700. Map 3, A8, p253* For afternoon tea. Hardly the grand affair you might imagine and not a cucumber sandwich within nibbling distance, but the small buffet table is crammed with cakes, scones, oodles of cream and a choice of half a dozen teas and four quality coffees. Sedate in a modest way, soft music in the background, and for 82kr a way of whiling away an hour or so.

Vesterbro and Frederiksberg

Restaurants

KKK Alberto K, *Radisson SAS Royal Hotel*, Hammerischsage, **T** 33426161. *Mon-Fri 1200-1500, Mon-Sat 1800-2400. Map 3, D3, p252* Exquisite Italian-Scandinavian cuisine on the 20th floor of the famous Jacobsen-designed hotel (see p127), using the cutlery that the architect (see p42) designed and his legendary Syveren (The Seven) chair. Panoramic views of the city (reserve a table on the town hall side) and a sybaritic six-course menu for 695kr: starters like cappuccino of green peas with fjord shrimps and chanterelles and dishes like truffle risotto and sautéed lobster, or a choice of dishes can be chosen (from 365-645kr). Lunch is a two-course affair; Italian wine list.

KK Flora Danica, Plaza Hotel, Bernstorffsgade 4, **T** 33939362. *Mon-Fri 0630-1000, 1200-2200, Sat-Sun 0730-1100, 1200-2200. Map 3, D4, p252* Roses dress the tables, orange plants, the windows and all set off with soft blue colours. As lunch spots go,

Flora Danica is hard to beat for a burger with smoked bacon and herb mayonnaise, steamed mussels in white wine, grilled chicken or duck breast and salad. After 1700, a dinner menu replaces the lunch one.
  ● *If leaving for the airport from Central Station for an early evening flight, walk next door to the* Plaza Hotel, *deposit your luggage and linger over lunch in here. For late evening flights, drop into the hotel's* Library Bar *for a last cocktail or two.*

★ **Restaurants to enjoy set wine menus**

Best
- La Crevette, p141
- Truffle Café, p142
- Søren K, p146
- Sult, p150
- Skt Gertruds Kloster, p148

KK Frascati, Vesterbrogade 9A, **T** 156690. *1000-2200. Map 3, D3, p252* Crisp, white tablecloths and clean colours define what is probably the best little Italian restaurant in the city, next to the Grand hotel. Excellent selection of appetizers, grilled scampi from Greenland and many other fine choices from a menu of seasonal pasta, fish and meat dishes.

KK Imperial Garden, Imperial Hotel, Vester Farimagsgade 9, **T** 33128000. *1200-2230. Map 3, D3, p252* Filled with natural greenery and a small pond, with above-average food if you're partial to roast beef with a sweet mustard sauce or pickled Baltic salmon, sliced and served from a trolley at the table. Service can be efficient to the point of briskness so ask to slow it down if necessary.

KK Passagens Spisehus, Vestrbrogade 42, **T** 33224757. *Mon 1800-2100, Tue-Thu 1800-2200, Fri-Sat 1700-2300. Map 3, E1, p252* Slightly chilly Nordic decor, with some singular choices like wild musk from Greenland, reindeer, and moose on the menu. The starters – roe of whitefish, dried cod, ray, Lapland carpaccio – are excellent; affordable set meals from 255kr; good wines, friendly and knowledgeable service, and a neat line in cocktails.

KK Vestauranten, DGI-byens Hotel, Tietgensgade 65, **T** 33298030. *1800-2230. Map 3, E4, p252* An old market, barn-like building, set menu (324kr) starts with a cocktail and three courses, or eat for less from the à la carte choices, while vegetarians could tuck into the buffet for under a 100kr. Starters like hot and cold artichokes, smoked salmon; main courses of fish, surf 'n' turf, lamb.

K Ban-Gaw, Istedgade 16, **T** 33228438. *1600-2300*. *Map 3, E2, p252* Situated opposite the Gay Centre shop, Ban-Gaw needs a facelift as regards its appearance and decor but the food has been recommended. King prawn vindaloo is 125kr.

K Bistro, Central Station, **T** 33692112. *1130-2200*. *Map 1, G8, p249* Not the only place to eat in the railway station for there are the usual schmuck franchises, but if you have a large appetite and want to eat Danish you could do worse than tuck into the eat-all-you-want buffet for 149kr.

K Bojesen, Værnedamsvej 10, **T** 33317055. *Mon-Fri and Sun 1200-2300, Sat 1100-2300*. *Map 3, D1, p252* Once a butcher's – the tiled floor and walls are original – and now an affordable place to enjoy lunch or dinner, plus a take-away section. Daily 95kr lunch specials are on a blackboard and the evening menu (not in English) kicks in at 1700.

● *Værnedamsvej is an interesting old street and there are a couple of patisseries – The Bagle Co and Marie-France – worth considering for a light lunch on the hoof or if planning a picnic.*

Cafés

K Bon Appetit, 15 Vesterbrogade, **T** 33311702. *Mon-Fri 0700-1600*. *Map 3, D2, p252* On the corner with Helgolandsgade, Bon Appetit has only a couple of bar stools to eat at and most customers are buying take-away rolls and *smørrebrød* for lunch; convenient to reach if staying in one of the Vesterbro hotels and fancying a light bite in your room.

K Café Sius, Rosenørns Allé, **T** 35356463. *Mon-Thu and Sun 1000-2400, Fri-Sat 1000-0200. Map 3, A1, p252* Coffees from Guatemala, Sumatra, Colombia, and Ethiopia at this usefully located licensed café for anyone staying in one of the Cab Inns (p131 and 132). The brunch, served until 1500 is 60kr but also salads, sandwiches, burgers, nachos. Outdoor tables, but close to the traffic.

K Café Sokkelund, Smallegade 36, **T** 38106400. *Mon-Sat 1000-2130, Sun 1000-1900. Map 2, B6, p252* Not too far from the Royal Copenhagen factory and in an area where there are none too many places for a decent lunch, the tapas plate of five different tapas for 56kr-85kr is worth a shout. Backgammon and chess can be played and there are occasionally evenings of live music.

K Det Gule Hus, 48 Istedgade, **T** 33259071. *1000-2400 (later at weekends). Map 3, F1, p252* A smart new café, indicative of Istedgade's changing social character, with polished wood floor and black and white 1950s photographs of the neighbourhood. The menu is in Danish but you can hardly go wrong with the range of brunches available up to 1400 each day for around 60kr. A handy joint to stop off for a coffee or quick meal if walking down Istedgade from your hotel.

K Hong Kong Grill, Gasværksvej 3, **T** 33213826. *1400-2330. Map 3, E1, p252* Handy joint for a quick bite if staying around Istedgade; Chinese take-aways, and burgers, with seats nearby in the garden of the *City Hostel*.

K Mexicansk Mad, Vesterbrogade 171, **T** 33254800. *Mon-Thu 1100-2100, Fri 1100-2200, Sat-Sun 1600-2200. Map 2, E8, p251* If feeling hungry after a visit to the Carlsberg brewery there is little to recommend by way of food in the area, but if you walk down the hill and turn right onto Vesterbrogade there is a small Mexican takeaway after a couple of hundred metres with one table inside.

A few doors down, the *Hos Robert* pub has an outside table where a takeaway could accompany another glass of the beer.

Around the Three Lakes

Restaurants

KK-K Pablo Picasso, Griffenfeldsgade 7, **T** 35343406. *Mon-Sun 1630-2200. Map 4, F1, p254* Prints of you-know-who on the wall alongside old black and white photographs of Copenhagen. The English menu features tapas and the house specialties are oven-grilled steak at 150kr and veal for 119kr, washed down with sangria at 22kr a glass.

K Govindas, Nørre Farimagsgade 82, **T** 33337444, www.govinds.dk *Mon-Sat 1200-2130. Map 4, H4, p254* Indian vegetarian buffet of nine different dishes for 59kr, and only 45kr for students and senior citizens. The restaurant is small, but not unduly cramped, and the service is friendly; no alcohol.

Cafés

K Café Lars Nørgård, Statens Museum for Kunst (Danish National Gallery), Sølvgade 48, **T** 33748494. *Tue-Sun 1000-1700, Wed 1000-2000. Map 4, G7, p255* Always a seductive range of cakes and pastries and a daily 98kr-brunch served between 1000 and 1400 in this stylish museum café. Sometimes dishes are inspired by current shows.

K Café og Ølhalle, Rømersgade 22, **T** 33932575. *Tue-Sun 1130-1600. Map 4, H5, p254* The restored 1892 setting of a worker's bar in the Arbejdermuseet (see p84) serves *smørrebrød* and daily specials around 40kr; similarly priced are the herrings –

★ **Fast food**

Best
- Jensen's Bøfhus, p143
- Felafel and pizza joints along Nørrebrogade, p158
- Shawarma and kebab places along Lower Strøget, p40
- Take-away *smørrebrød* from bakeries
- Thai food at Aløj Dee, p144

salted, marinated or spiced – the spare ribs, liver pâté or meatballs. Stjerne Pilsner, as brewed at the Workers' Brewery Stjerne, to wash it down with.

K Ma Ma, Nørrebrogade 98, **T** 35360775. *1100-2300. Map 4, D1, p254 Ma Ma*, on the corner with Sjællandsgade, is just one of the many small takeaways dispensing shawarma (a very soft pitta bread), felafel and pizza along Nørrebrogade between the cemetery and the lakes. Whatever you eat is likely to cost between 10kr and 40kr and makes for a possible picnic in Assistens Kirkegård.

K Pastamania, Vendersgade 16, **T** 33914060. *Mon-Fri 1000-2200, Sat-Sun 1200-2200. Map 4, H4, p254* Only a couple of tables at this small pizza and pasta joint but always good for a takeaway, and handy if staying in one of the nearby hotels. A choice of 28 pizzas averaging around 65kr, pizza slices for half that price, salads, pasta dishes, sandwiches, pitta bread and burgers.

K Props Coffee Shop, Blågårdsgade 5, **T** 35369955. *Mon-Wed 1100-2400, Thu-Sat 1100-0200. Sun 1200-2300. Map 4, G2, p254 Hygee* (p191) is the karma late at night when jazz music is playing and the candles come out to cast light around the calm, bare wood decor. The food, with specials chalked up on a blackboard opposite the bar, comes from the *Shark House* next door (p159). Outdoor tables, and coffee only 10kr.

K Pussy Galore's Flying Circus, Sankt Hans Torv, **T** 35245300, www.pussy-galore.dk *Mon-Fri 0800-0200, Sat-Sun 0900-0200. Map 4, E2, p254 See also p175*   The stereotype of a modern Copenhagen café, with Arne Jacobsen (p42) chairs, minimalist decor and heavily accented fusion food. Similar in style to *Sebastopol* (see below) with indoor and outdoor tables, and a regular crowd of chic creative types, and with the added punch of the Pussy Galore cocktail (vodka, jordbærlikør, brut and Cinzano).

K Sebastopol, Sankt Hans Torv, **T** 35363002, www.sebastopol.dk *Mon-Wed and Sun 0800-0100, Thu-Sat 0800-0200. Map 4, E2, p254* A brasserie-style hangout for wannabes, especially in summer when a tendency to pose lightens up the scene around the outdoor tables, but always good for a bite to eat and a bottle of Singha or Newcastle Brown. A reliable choice of wines, brunch, omelettes, salads, sandwiches, desserts, meals from 80kr and *plat du jour* around 100kr.

K Shark House Deli, Blågårdsgade 3, **T** 35355135. *Mon-Fri 1100-2100, Sat 1100-1900. Map 4, G2, p254* Great for a quick meal in Nørrebro, day or night – on your left shortly after turning into Blågårdsgade off Nørrebrogade. The sandwiches, from a little over 30kr to nearly 50kr, are some of the munchiest anywhere in the city. The Shark House Chili for 60kr is another firm favourite.

Christiania and around

Restaurants

KKK Era Ora, Overgaden Neden Vandet 33B, **T** 32540693. *Mon-Sat 1200-1500, 1800-2400. Map 3, E9, p253* Michelin-star Italian restaurant in an unlikely setting on the fringe of Christianshavn. Home-made pasta, of course, veal and venison

★ **Picnic places**

Best

- Kongens Have (Royal Garden), p71
- Canal-side with the Black Diamond leaning towards you, p54
- Frederiksberg Have, p78
- Lakeside at Frederiksborg Slot, p78
- Assistens Kirkegård, p85

may feature, always fresh fish. Superb food but do be aware that the pricing of drinks can be confusing – keep an eye on the tab.

KKK Base Camp, Halvtolv Bygningen 148, **T** 70232318. *Wed-Thu 1800-0100, Fri-Sat 1100-1700. Closed on Mon and Thu between Oct- May. Bus no 8 stops close by this huge eatery that seats up to 600. Map 3, F12, p253* Using its setting as a former military workshop for repairing naval cannon to good effect, *Base Camp* resembles a stage set for an episode of MASH. Main courses on the fusion- inspired menu are about 150kr and the hearty Sunday brunch for 90kr attracts Copenhageners.

KK-K Spiseloppen, Bådmandsstræde 43, Christiania, **T** 32579558. *Tue-Sun 1700-2200. Map 3, C12, p253* Take the right turn off Pusher Street and go up the ramshackle stairs in the Loppen building for a delightful change of decor – low-ceilinged, designed in wood and reasonable prices to boot. Christiania's best restaurant by a long shot, with consistently above-average food. Menus change regularly but expect fusion-inspired dishes.

! There's no rush for a rasher of bacon in Denmark. There are more pigs in this porcine-friendly land than there are people. The population of nearly 5.5 million is outnumbered by nearly four times as many hogs trotting in at 20 million!

K Morgenstedet, Langgaden, Christiania. *1200-2100. To find Morgenstedet, walk down Pusher St and take a left down past Månefiskeren and it's on your left. Map 3, C12, p253* Once famous for its breakfasts served to ravers in the 1970s, *Morgenstedet* is a reliable eatery for vegetarians – meals around 50kr – with the salads and bean stews laid out to view and tables inside or out on a gravelled garden area. Smoking nor alcohol is allowed.

Cafés

K Månefiskeren, Fremtidsskoven, Christiania. *Tue-Sun 1000-0100. Map 3, C12, p253* Hard to miss this colourful-looking café in the heart of Christiania, look for a man on the moon figure with a fishing rod and a joint. Snooker tables, chessboards and spliffs. Light meals, good for a breakfast or cake and sandwiches any time. Note the signs, warning visitors to beware of pickpockets.

Around Copenhagen

Helsingør

K Kammercaféen, Havneplasdsen 1, **T** 49282052. *0900-1800.* Near to the station, in the customs house building behind the tourist office, this café is fine for a coffee or a light meal. The café in the railway station itself is pleasant enough and offers quick meals like goulash for under 50kr.

K Ophelia, *Hotel Hamlet*, Bramstræde 5, **T** 49210591. *1030-2100.* The Shakespeare connection is not milked to death in Helsingør so the occasional name-dropping is forgivable. A pleasant hotel restaurant where a comfortable *smørrebrød* lunch can be enjoyed, or an evening meal of traditional Danish dishes.

K Rådmand Davids Hus, Strandgade 70,
T 49261043. *0900-2000*. Cross over the road from the railway
station, walk up Brostræde by the tourist office and Strandgade
runs across at the next intersection, with *Rådmand Davids Hus* to
the left. The daily lunch of traditional Danish fare is good value at
around 70kr.

K World, Bramstræde 1, **T** 49201126. *1130-2300*. Opposite
Helsingør's railway station, the *World* certainly looks like a Chinese
restaurant and so does the menu, although there are some
concessions to non-Oriental tastes like the Irish coffee that rounds
off the special menu for two people, 118kr each.

Roskilde

KK-K Raadhuskælderen, Stændertorvet, Roskilde, **T** 46360100,
www.raadhuskælderen.com *1130-1600, 1700-2200*. With
15th-century cellar rooms, bare red brick walls, porches and vaults
still visible, *Raadhuskælderen* can muster some atmosphere at
night. Lunch could be herrings, onions and capers, or plaice,
asparagus and caviar at one of the garden tables; dinner has main
courses like smoked pork, or home-made lobster bisque laced with
cognac for 88kr.

KK-K Snekken, Viking Ship Museum, Vindeboder 16, Roskilde,
T 46359816, www.snekken.dk *1130-2100*. Large and airy,
glass-fronted restaurant with outdoor tables facing the fjord and
a jazzy restaurant inside serving dishes like veal carpaccio with
couscous and Parmesan (74kr), veal and grilled mango and foie
gras sauce (188kr), and cold rhubarb with elderflower soup and
pistachio ice cream. Lunch, until 1600, includes a tasty salad and
salmon for 68kr, or the Snekken plate with four kinds of specialties
for 108kr.

Hillerød

KK Brasserie Kong Christian, Slotsgade 59, **T** 48245350, www.brasserie-kong-christian.dk *1000-2200*. Lunch and dinner menus at reasonable prices. Outdoor tables in the summer, with castle views, but the interior is not too exiting.

KK El Castillo's Cantina, Slotsgade 61, **T** 48261911. *1600-2300*. A comfortable cantina-style setting of bright colours with a hanging Mexican carpet and brass lamps. A set meal is about 130kr. If the opening time is inconvenient, try *Hennessy's* Irish pub down the street.

Malmö

KK-K Izakaya Koi, Lilla Torg 5, **T** 6112020. *Mon-Thu 1130-0100, Fri-Sat 1700-0200, Sun 1700-0100*. Authentic Japanese cuisine but expect some surprises, like cheese and guacamole in the sushi. Prices average about 200kr per person; outdoor tables in the summer and DJ music inside at weekends.

KK-K Johan P, Lilla Torg, **T** 971818. *Mon-Fri 1000-1800, Sat 1000-1600*. Inside Saluhallen, a food centre on the corner of the square, *Johan P* is a consistently good fish restaurant with meals from 70kr.

KK Thott's, *Radisson SAS Hotel*, Östergatan 10, **T** 6984800. *1200-2200*. Cosy setting in a building that dates back to the 1550s, good-value set meals at 245/265kr for two/three courses, and some decent wines.

Eating and drinking

The Danes are seriously sociable, so it is no surprise to find that the city boasts a large, ever-changing bar and club scene to meet the demands of a major European style-capital. The division between café, bar and club are somewhat blurred as most establishments are hybrid and metamorphe into each of them as the night progresses. It is not uncommon for a low-key brunch café to welcome an early evening lounge crowd in search of alcohol and a chillfactor and then pick up the pace with DJs playing until the early hours of the morning. Delicatessen, Krasnapolsky and Bang & Jensen are all good examples of this. Copenhageners don't start to kick their heels until at least 2400-0100, particularly at weekends, but stylish Scandinavian-style lounge bars (Ideal Bar, see p172, and Stereo Bar, see p175, among the best) with a warm, intimate and inviting atmosphere will keep you simmering until then.

There is no one definitive area for nightlife, but everything pretty much centres around Vesterbro, Nørrebro, Østerbro and the City. The great thing is that they are all close enough to sample a selection from several of them in any one night either by foot, city bike, or a short cab ride. Special one-off and try-out club and bar nights are plentiful, which makes the scene difficult to stay abreast of.Most bars and cafes stock a good range of promotional flyers and free newspapers that are worth checking out before you make a start. The weekly *Copenhagen Post's In & Out* guide contains a good day-by-day rundown in English.

Rådhuspladsen and around

Bars

Azhiba, Læderstræde 32, **T** 33135060. *Mon-Thu 1200-2400, Fri-Sat 1200-0100. Map 3, C6, p252* Meaning 'fantastic' in Arabic, it's just that. The decor and ambience is Nordic Africa meets Denmark. The Danish design within is rendered in natural materials (stone, wood, leather) and colours (sandy and earthy browns). Very loungey feel with self-conscious but unpretentious crowd. Well-stocked bar at city prices.

Aura, Rådhusstræde 4, **T** 33365060. *Fri-Sat 1100-0300. Map 3, C6, p252* Weekend-only cocktail bar (restaurant at other times) with lounge music and a sophisticated affluent crowd. Serve around 20 of their own cocktails. Chic, minimalist decor.

Drop Inn, Kompagnistræde 34, **T** 33112404. *Until 0500 daily. Map 3, C6, p252* This large bar entertains a relaxed middle-of-the road crowd with live jazz- and folk-inspired music. The frontage opens up in the summer months and tables spill out onto the quaint pavements and make it a very desirable option and welcome break from other hyper-cool hangouts. Cheap beer before 1900, reasonable prices thereafter.

Krasnapolsky, Vestergade 10, **T** 33328800. *Mon-Wed 1000-0200, Thu-Sat 1000-0500, Sun 1400-2400. Map 3, C6, p252* Debuted in the 80s and caused a frenzy, and still going pretty strong. Chilled and low-key during the week but kicks into life Thu-Sat when DJs play R&B, funk and disco until 0500. Needs a facelift and less ambitious bar prices, but that doesn't seem to have waned it's popularity thus far. Local artist exhibit on the walls and are often very good.

Mojo, Løngangstræde 21C, **T** 33116453. *Daily 2000-0500. Map 3, C6, p252* Live blues everynight along with cheap draught beer between 2000-2200. Mixed late-20s, early-30s crowd. Extremely smoky, small and grubby, but always rammed the rafters – just as a blues joint should be.

Peder Oxe's Vinkælder, Gråbrødretorv 11, **T** 33111193. *Until 0100 daily. Map 3, B6, p252* A cavernous, atmospheric, cosy cellar bar that serves up a good range of wines and cocktails amidst good world, latin and funk beats. A hidden ambient gem.

Clubs

Barfly & Britannia, Løvstræde 4, **T** 33148969. *Wed-Thu 2200-0500, Fri 2100-0500, Sat 2100-0600. Map 3, B6, p252* An entertainment temple over six levels. The groundfloor bar and basement disco are both tuned into a 70s, 80s and 90s soundtrack to cater for a 30-something crowd. Dance, light techno and britpop are the flavour of the third-floor club which attracts a younger crowd.

Copenhagen Jazzhouse, Niels Hemmingsens Gade 10, **T** 33932616. *Thu-Sat 2400-0500. 60kr (free Thu). Map 3, B7,* *p253* Post-concert club nights for a fresh-faced crowd who revel and flirt to the eclectic latin, house, acid jazz, oldschool-disco, bossa nova, R&B and soul sets from popular residential DJs. Not particularly cool, but very fun.

IN, Nørregade 1, **T** 33117478. *Thu 2300-0600, Fri 2300-0800, Sat 2300-1000. 50-150kr. Map 3, C5, p252* Debauched creche for young crowd into banging (Euro)house and (Euro)trance. Dubious entrance policies include drink as much draught beer, wine and champagne (fizzy wine) for a very small blanket fee and 'girls go cheaper' to entice the boys. Good light/laser shows. Attracts big-name live acts, such as Sash and Ian Van Dahl.

Level CPH, Skindergade 45-47, **T** 33132625. *Fri-Sat 2300-0500. 60 Kr. Map 3, C6, p252* Lush lighting, stylish chillout rooms and vibrant dance areas. An appreciative crowd soak up predominately house sounds. Welcomes guest DJs from international clubland every weekend. Also has some good Danish resident DJs. Look out for special club nights.

Sabor Latino, Vester Voldgade 85, **T** 33119766. *Thu 2100-0300, Fri-Sat 2100-0500. Map 3, D6, p252* Salsa club offering lessons at 2200-2300 before the disco kicks off at 2400. Energetic Latinos brush-up their moves among a diverse enthusiastic Danish crowd. Authentic and fun. Good-priced cocktails.

Q House of Dance, Axeltorv 5, **T** 33111915. *Fri-Sat 2300-0600. Map 3, C3, p252* Formerly Daddy's, this basement club claims to be the first to have imported disco to Denmark. Commercial dance for a young, gregarious and often leery crowd. Four bars, including a cocktail bar and shot bar. TV monitors link the male and female toilets (unbelievably tacky, but true) and add to the sharking atmosphere.

Bars and clubs

Slotsholmen and around

Bars

Luftkastellet, Strandgade 100B, **T** 32540369. *Map 3, C10, p253*
Translates as 'Castle in the Air'. An unused harbour area transformed
into a very hip beach bar with sand on the waterfront and a
high-ceiling warehouse restaurant. Expect anything from jazz and
dub, to indian and soft house. Seasonal opening.

Nyhavn and around

Bars

Andy's Bar, Gothersgade 33B, **T** 33124685. *Until 0500 daily. Map
3, A8, p253* Run-down nightbar with a traditional pub atmosphere
and interior. A wateringhole for a mixed crowd – from urban
hipsters to hardened drinkers. No other place like it town.

Bo-Bi Bar, Klareboderne 14, **T** 33125543. *Map 3, A7, p253* Well-
kept bar with a definite pub feel. Jazz is played as a background to
conversation. Relaxed place to meet friends and socialise among a
strange mix of a young arty bohemian clientele and older men who
like a fine whisky.

Dan Turell, Store Regnegade 3-5, **T** 33141047. *Mon-Tue
0900-2400, Wed 0900-0100, Thu 0900-0200, Fri-Sat 0900-0400,
Sun 1000-2400. Map 3, A8, p253* A favourite of fashion-conscious
media types and wannabes. Its many windows, mirrored walls and
lack of intimate corners create a goldfish bowl effect that may not
be for the shy or retiring. Expensive bar prices, but lively and
entertaining. A great people-watching experience to be had.

Fisken, Nyhavn 27, **T** 33119906. *Mon-Thu 0900-0300, Fri-Sat 0900-0500, Sun 0900-0200. Map 3, A9, p253* Tatty nautical cellar bar/pub situated in the tourist trap of Nyhavn (New Harbour). Fishing nets and fishing paraphernalia decorate the walls, ceilings and any other available space. Unlike the other offerings along this stretch, it has unique charm and warmth. Live music, usually folky, every evening. Neither trendy or typically Danish, but very very cosy and inviting.

Zoo Bar, Kronprinsensgade 7, **T** 33156869. *Mon-Wed. Map 3, A7, p253* Cool two-room hangout. Serves its own Zoo burger, which is very good, along with other basic snacks until 2100 (2200 on Fri). DJs turn out impressive funk-groove sets that keep it filled to the brim Thu-Sat.

Clubs

Cavi, Lille Kongensgade 16, **T** 33112020. *Thu-Fri 2300-0500, Sat 2300-0600. 50Kr Thu-Fri, 100kr Sat (free for women all nights). Map 3, B8, p253* R&B, two step, commercial house and hip hop club with a sociable mixed crowd. Bellowing sheets hang from the ceilings amidst candlelit tables where you can chat and get intimate during a break from the lively dancefloor. The outdoor terrace with its own bar.

Vesterbro and Fredriksberg

Bars

Bang & Jensen Istedgade 130, **T** 33255318. *Mon-Fri 0800-0200, Sat 1000-0200, Sun 1000-2400. Map 2, F12, p251* A long-standing institution (converted chemist) on Istedgade that is home-from-home for many locals who flock to revel in its rundown kitsch familiarity and enjoy brunch. Busy pre-clubbing bar at weekends, and around the clock during summer months when it expands onto the streets.

Delicatessen, Vesterbrogade 120, **T** 33221633. *Mon-Wed 1100-2400, Thu-Sat 1100-0300, Sun 1100-2400. Map 2, E10, p251* Beautifully concrete and stark by design with an impressive metallic buffed bar. Fashionable eaterie/hangout that serves a good range of drinks, including mid-priced (50-60Kr) cocktails. Thursday to Saturday a pre-clubbing crowd ascend to warm-up to ambient and funky sounds from local DJs.

Ideal Bar, Enghavevej 40, **T** 33 25 70 11. *Wed 1800-0200, Thu 1800-0400, Fri-Sat 1800-0500. Map 2, F11, p251* Extremely popular hangout which is part of the Vega outfit. Friendly music- and fashion-conscious Vesterbrø crowd. The layout and interior is loungey with a small dancefloor. Latin, world and funk sets. Big queues from 1200 at weekends.

Märkbar, Vesterbrogade 106A, **T** 33212393. *Mon-Wed 1500-0200, Thu-Sat 1500-0500. Map 2, E12, p251* Cosy cellar bar serving a good selection of beers and speciality drinks, such as TV-Bingo and the very expensive (180Kr) but lethal Blietzkrieg (Tequila, Gin, Rum, Starka Vodka, Blue Bols plus mixers). Happy hour between 2000-2100 when you can grab two Budvar for 30kr. On the sound front, expect Nick Cave and German alternative rock.

Obelix, Vesterbrogade 53, **T** 33313414. *Daily 0830-0200. Map 3, E1, p252* Welcoming cartoon-themed bar overlooking Vesterbro Torv (square). Nothing fancy or adventurous, but a relaxed place to meet and chat with a beer.

Riesen, Oehlenschlägersgade 36, **T** 33230734. *Thu-Sat 2000-0200. Map 2, F12, p251* Small and simple bar filled with local boys and bar stools, both fall over as the night progresses. Old classics and overlooked films are run on the ceiling TV, while music is only ever background. Good selection of alcohol and drinks at low prices. A White Russian will set you back 40Kr.

Riga, Istedgade 79, **T** 33252560. *Tue-Wed 1500-0100, Thu-Sun 1100-0100. Map 3, F1, p252* Small shabby bar popular with a chilled arty west end crowd and local Istedgade residents. A spinning glitter ball hanging between the two back lounge rooms are as elegant as it gets, but the threadbare comfy sofas are part of the charm. Basic, inexpensive bar.

Clubs

Vega, Enghavevej 40, **T** 33257011. *Fri-Sat 1100-0500 plus special nights. Map 2, F11, p254* A renovated 50s trade union building is home to one of the most exciting and cool clubbing experience in Copenhagen. Ever-changing club nights spanning anything from electronic to deep house. They are as serious about cutting-edge music and sound systems as they are about cool Scandinavian interior design. Clientele are aspirational but inoffensive.

Around the Three Lakes

Bars

Bankerât, Ahlefeldtsgade 29, **T** 33936988. *Until 2400 daily. Map 3, A3, p252* Perfect place to start an evening. Beamed ceilings and candlelight contribute to the relaxed look and feel, which is a far cry from the mid-90s sterile bar concept. Sun at 2100 during the winter season they show big screen movies.

Barcelona, Fælledvej 21, **T** 35357611. *Mon-Wed 1100-0200, Thu-Sun 1100-0500. Map 4, F2, p254* An alternative to city bars and clubs. Attracts a spirited crowd who drink and dance the weekend away to DJs spinning light soul and funk. Bit outdated musically and stylistically.

Bibendum, Nansensgade 45, **T** 33330774. *Map 3, A3, p252* Relaxed but lively rustic-style wine bar serving tapas and some of the finest wine imports. 50 varieties by the glass and 100 by the bottle. Staff are warm and welcoming, as is the atmosphere. Worth calling beforehand to book a table and avoid disappointment.

Bopa, Bopa Plads, **T** 35430566. *Mon-Tue 1030-0100, Wed 1030-0300, Thu-Sat 1030-0500, Sun 1000-2400. Map 4, A7, p255* Simplistic rustic-style and mainstream uplifting sounds make it a nice pit-stop. Particularly charming in the summer when the clientele are enticed from the small interior dancefloor to chill, chat, sip and flirt outside on rugs and deckchairs.

Barstarten, Kapelvej 1, **T** 35241100. *Mon-Wed 1200-2400, Thu-Sat 1200-0300, Sun 1000-2200. Map 4, F1, p254* Uninspiring mini-malistic decor and ambience during the week, but the temperature rises along with the sound levels Thursday to Satur day when a pre-clubbing crowd gather to enjoy soul and funk DJ sets.

Kruts Karport, Øster Farimagsgade 12, **T** 35268638. *Map 4, F6, p254* French-inspired bar serving foreign beers, Absinth (few Danish bars do) and Denmarks biggest selection of speciality whisky (special whisky nights hosted during winter months).

Mexi Bar, Elmegade 27, **T** 35377766. *Map 4, E2, p254* Crass but fun Mexican themed bar. Grass hut entrance, fairy lights on mass and illuminated stars adorn the ceiling. Cut-cost cocktails lead to a rowdy party atmosphere into the early hours.

Morgans, Elmegade 15, **T** 35352672. *Map 4, E2, p254* Low-key American dineresque bar complete with cushioned red leatherette benches and a pink ambient backlight. Good range of smoothies, cocktails and bar food. Eclectic, non-intrusive lounge music permits conversation.

Pavillionen i Fælledparken, Borgmester Jensens Allé 45, **T** 35387393. *Map 4, B4, p254* Seasonal outdoor picnic-style seating, heating and bar points in leafy park surroundings centred around a pavilion dancefloor filled with pop and happy house. Predatory crowd.

Pussy Galore's Flying Circus, Sankt Hans Torv 30, **T** 35245300. *Until 0200 daily*. *Map 4, E2, p254 See also p159* Quintessential 'less is more' Danish design (Jacobsen chairs throughout) and a large selection of reasonably-priced spirits. Attracts stylish urbanites who come to relax and take it easy. Conducive to striking-up conversation (and more) with interesting locals who have their finger on the pulse.

Sebastopol, Sankt Hans Torv 32, **T** 35363002. *Mon-Wed 0800-0100, Thu-Sat 0800-0200, Sun 0800-0100. Map 4, E2, p254* Parisian elegance and charm. Tables spill onto the square in summer months when trendy, young professional flock to drink until the early hours following superb gastronomic delights served up earlier in the evening. Popular meeting point for Rust nightclubbers at weekends, which is just around the corner.

Stereo Bar Linnesgade 16A, **T** 33136113. *Wed-Sat 2000-0300. Map 4, H5, p254* Subdued 60s and 70s decor and lighting and a relaxed but stylish loungey clientele put Stereo bar firmly on the must-go map. Funky easy listening and an impressive range of exotic cocktails and tipples dominate the main bar, while the intimate cellar club is an eclectic sound station inhabited by pretty good Denmark DJs who deliver anything from house, trip hop, drum and bass and electronic sets that are usually edgy and fresh.

Clubs

Park, Østerbrogade 79, **T** 35 42 62 48. *Thu-Sat 2300-0500. Map 4, A7, p255* Formerly the function rooms of the national stadium (Parken), this 2,000 capacity, three-dancefloor club offering pulls in a loyal, party-going crowd. Ostentatious decor includes chandeliers hanging from 1920s high ceilings and mirrored walls and ceilings. Mainstream disco, pop and happy house. Live music Sun-Wed in the cosy ground floor Kitty Club. Expect big queues at the weekend.

Rust, Guldbergsgade 8, **T** 35245200. *Living Room Wed-Sat 2100-0500; Basement Fri-Sat 0100-0500; Main Bar Wed-Sat 0000-0500; 30-50kr. Map 4, E2, p254* Rust is the cornerstone of the city's DJ and club culture. Rivalling Vega, it is spread over three floors. The Living Room is a super-cool mellow cocktail lounge with 70s-meets-millennium style. The Bassment is the engine room for a range of weekend club nights. The Main Bar (with seating, standing and dance areas) plays host to live acts, ranging from international DJs to Danish rock outfits.

Stengade 30 Stengade 18, **T** 35360938. *Tue-Wed 2100-0200, Thu-Sat 2200-0500. Map 4, G1, p254* Grundgy and dark three-floor venue attracting an alternative crowd. Danish and European rock and experimental dance. A popular venue to catch live up-and-coming local musicians and DJs, but can be very hit and miss. Various club nights.

Denmark has always benefited from a thriving arts scene and Copenhagen is very much a one-stop-shop for film, dance, music and theatre.

Danes are very proud of their own film industry and output. Dogma, an artistic/cinematic movement spearheaded by Lars Von Trier with strict rules and techniques aimed at changing the sensational 'trickery' of film-making in favour of the reality of character and situation, firmly re-established Denmark on the international film map during the late 90s. Film plays a seminal role in the entertainment calendar of most Copenhageners. Their appetite for the big screen is reflected in the number and popularity of cinemas throughout the city, both multiplexes and art-house cinemas. With more than 100 rock, folk and jazz festivals every year, and a growing international concert scene, Copenhagen is buzzing on the live-music front, and generally has something for everyone all year round. The fringe theatre and dance scenes, unlike their European counterparts, are revered for their innovation rather than scorned as the poor relation to the grand theatres that play host to big productions.

Cinema

All movies in Denmark are screened in their original language with Danish subtitles (children's films are often dubbed). Ticket prices range from 40-85kr.

Cinemateket, Gothersgade 55, **T** 33743412. *Map 4, H7, p255*
Three-screen complex affiliated with the Danish Film Institute. A gem for film connoisseurs. Repertoire of classic, foreign, documentary, art, short and alternative films, plus special children's films. Bookstore sells seminal texts and criticism, posters, videos and DVDs. Also houses a comprehensive documentary archive and a good café.

CinemaxX Fisketorvet, Fisketorvet Shopping Center, **T** 70101202. *Map 3, H3, p252* Ten-screen multiplex. Mostly Danish and American big releases.

Dagmar Teatret, Jernbanegade 2, **T** 33143222. *Map 3, C4, p252* Five screens showing American and European films.

Empire Bio, Guldbergsgade 29F, **T** 35360036. *Map 4, E1, p254* One of the best cinemas in Copenhagen situated in the urban-chic of Nørrebro (Sankt Hans Torv just around the corner for post-film drinks and food) . Four screens (largest is a 600-seater) showing mainly European and Danish releases. Exquisite comfort with up to 1.5 m legroom and double arm rests. Double seats on the back row for the romantic.

Gloria, Rådhuspladsen 59, **T** 33124292. *Map 3, C5, p252* Independent and bohemian. Charming one-screen (106-seater) cinema showing mainly independent American and European films.

Grand Teatret, Mikkel Bryggers Gade 8, **T** 33151611. *Map 3, C5, p252* The city's oldest cinema. Six screens showing European (mainly French, English and Scandinavian) and American 'serious' films for an intellectual cinema-going audience.

Husets Biograf, Magstræde 14, **T** 33324077. *Map 3, C6, p252* Small (57 seats) and cosy art-house cinema showing indies (from Asian and Hong-Kong flicks to USA and European output). Old-style wooden seats with own tables.

Imperial, Ved Vesterport 4, **T** 70131211. *Map 3, C3, p252* The city's biggest and most expensive (60-85Kr). One screen (it's a monster) that can welcome over 1,000 guests per screening (and it often does). Mainly premier Hollywood blockbusters. Comfortable seats, good legroom, air conditioning and sensational THX-sound system.

Palads, Axeltorv 9, **T** 70131211. *Tickets 40-65Kr. Map 3, C3, p252* The multi-coloured multiplex with 17 screens (biggest has 689 seats). Good range of American releases, from romantic comedies to action.

Palladium, Vesterbrogade 1 C, **T** 70131211. *Map 3, D4, p252* Three-screen cinema popular with an 'adult' audience. Predominately big American and English films.

Park Bio, Østerbrogade 79, **T** 35383362. *Map 4, A6, p254* One-screen cinema with a 243 capacity. Shows good variety of post-premier English and American movies, as well as a selection of foreign films. Café selling film posters.

Posthus-Teatret, Rådhusstræde 1, **T** 33116611. *Map 3, C6, p252* The city's best art-house offering good experimental European films.

Vester Vov Vov, Absalonsgade 5, **T** 33244200. *Map 3, E1, p252*
Two 70-seater screens with novel airplane seating complete with
attached tables for beverages. Show a good range of European
and American indies.

Comedy

Denmark humour is black, satirical and ironic. Unfortunately, most
of it can't be shared as it's nearly always delivered in Danish and
there isn't much of a comedy circuit to speak of. However, there
are a couple of gems that may tickle your fancy.

Comedy Zoo, Kompagnistræde 19, **T** 38881952,
www.stand-up.dk/zoo.html *Map 3, C6, p252* Copenhagen's
premier comedy venue with nightly shows spanning improv,
sketches and stand-up (often in English). Dinner and show combo
tickets available. Friday and Saturday shows followed by Zoo
Clubbing with DJs picking up the fun where the shows left off.

Crazy Christmas Cabaret, London Toast Theatre, **T** 33228686,
www.londontoast.dk Hugely successful English theatre company,
founded by Vivienne McKee, who have pulled in packed houses
with their wacky annual Christmas cabaret shows (November to
December) for the last two decades. Expect panto-style audience
participation, puns, gags and song. Staged at Tivoli's Glassalen
Theatre for the last five years. Venue subject to change, so check
for details.

Dance

In terms of 'traditional' ballet, there isn't as much as you'd expect,
and it's pretty much monopolized by Den Gamle Scene (The Old
Stage) of Det Kongelige Teater (The Royal Theatre). It often plays
host to the Royal Ballet and good international companies and

classical performances. The Peter Schaufuss Ballet company often puts in regular appearances at Det Ny Teater and, as it is responsible for the development of contemporary ballet in Denmark, should not be missed. Experimental and contemporary dance is plentiful, although, like most European capitals, companies are subject to harsh funding and subsequently come and go very quickly. The Nyt Dansk Danse Teater (NDDT) has very much been the company responsible for the development of contemporary dance in Denmark since its inception over two decades ago (formerly known as the Patterson Project). Tim Rushton is currently at its helm as artistic director and it produces around 70 performances per year and benefits from many international collaborations.

Dansescenen, Østerfælled Torv 34, **T** 35435858, www.dansescenen.dk *Map 4, A6, p254* Copenhagen's seminal dance venue. Attracts performances by prolific international and home-grown companies (NDDT often frequent the stage).

Det Ny Teatre, Gammel Kongevej 29, **T** 33255075, www.detnyteater.dk *Map 3, D1, p252* Regular contemporary family-orientated ballet productions, often by the Peter Schaufuss Ballet company.

Kanonhallen, Østerfælled Torv 37, **T** 35432021, www.kanonhallen.net *Map 4, A6, p254* Outstanding repertoire of Danish and European contemporary/experimental dance.

Tivoli Koncertsal/Plænen, Vesterbrogade 3, **T** 33151001. *Map 3, D4, p252* Two Tivoli stages that often welcome the Royal Ballet and high-quality dance performances.

Music

Jazz

The city has a worldwide reputation for jazz that came into its own during the 60s and 70s when a wave of international names, such as Dexter Gordon and Ben Webster, set up home in Copenhagen. Denmark also boasts a few international jazz talents of its own – The Doky Brothers and Hans Ulrik, among others. The city comes to life with street performances and live music almost everywhere during the annual Copenhagen Jazz Festival (see p191), while the blue notes of well-known jazz venues attract crowds throughout the year.

Many bars and cafes often have good one-off live performances from local jazz talent that are also well worth keeping your eyes peeled for. For rock and pop events, the city has an ever-growing collection of venues that seem to be undergoing constant facelifts and improvements to compete as pitstops for prolific musicians on European and international tours.

Copenhagen JazzHouse, Niels Hemmingsens Gade 10, **T** 33154700, www.jazzhouse.dk *Map 3, B7, p253* Live jazz from local and international talent. Thursday to Saturday only.

La Fontaine, Kompagnistræde 11, **T** 33116098. *Map 3, C6, p252* Intimate (capacity 60) jazz club legendary for its nocturnal jam sessions.

Concert venues

Amager Bio, Øresundvej 6, **T** 70156565. This 1,000-capacity converted cinema has recently attracted Bryan Ferry and Marianne Faithful. Intimate with great acoustics. Just out of the city.

Den Grå Hal, Christiania, **T** 32543135. From indie (Portishead) to legends (Bob Dylan), this is a seminal live-music venue that dates back to the 70s with the evolution of the free-state of Christiania.

Forum, Julius Thomsens Plads 1, **T** 32472000. *Map 3, A1, p252* Concert and exhibition hall attracting such big international names as Kylie and Destiny's Child.

KB Hallen, Peter Bangs Vej 147, **T** 38714150. *Map 2, C1, p250* Sports centre circa 1876, home to København FC and many big-name rock and pop concerts.

Parken, Øster Alle 50, **T** 35433131. *Map 4, A5, p250* Awesome 41,000-capacity national stadium with retractable roof. Think Michael Jackson, Rolling Stones, Tina Turner, Robbie Williams.

Pumpehuset, Studiestræde 52, **T** 33931960. A 600-capacity venue often showcasing local rock, pop and indie talents gaining momentum.

Vega, Enghavevej 40, **T** 33257011, www.vega.dk *Map 2, F10, p251* Located in the urban chic of Vesterbro, this seminal live-music venue with a capacity of 1500 has attracted the likes of Bowie, Bjork and Prince.

Opera

Copenhagen is currently raising the profile of opera with the building of a new opera house at Holmen, close to the city centre. Until the grand opening, scheduled for 2005, the city's operatic repertoire centres around two, very different, key venues.

Den Anden Opera, Kronprinsengade 7, T 33323830, www.denandenopera.dk *Map 3, A7, p253* 'The Other Opera' is the

Arts and entertainment

small (100 capacity) home of contemporary chamber opera. Since 1995 it has continually commissioned and produced two to three new works every season. Experimental and explosive.

Det Kongelige Teater, Gamle Scenen, Kongens Nytorv, **T** 33696969, www.kgl-teater.dk *Map 3, B8, p253* The Old Stage at the Royal Theatre stages regular worldclass performances in a more traditional vein. Very popular, so purchase tickets well in advance.

Theatre

Despite its lack of traditional training ground, Copenhagen has a lively theatre scene that spans classical drama to experimental performance art. Plays are predominately performed in Danish. The experimental fringe scene attracts practioners from around the world and often combines narrative, poetry, dance, multimedia and physical theatre, which makes it more accessible to a non Danish-speaking audiences and often culminates in ground-breaking performances.

Betty Nansen Teatret, Frederiksberg Alle 57, **T** 33211490, www.bettynansen.dk *Map 2, D9, p251* Newly interpreted classics along with modern Scandinavian drama and musicals. Predominately performed in Danish.

Cafe Teatret, Skindergade 3, **T** 33125814, www.cafeteatret.dk *Map 3, A3, p252* Three stages showing some of the best experimental performance art. Varied repertoire that often encompasses cabaret, improvisation and world theatre. A hub of everything new and innovative since the 1960s.

Det Kongelige Teater, **T** 33696969, www.kgl-teater.dk The Royal Theatre has a commitment to a varied artistic programme that encompasses drama, opera and ballet. It has three main performance sites. The Gamle Scenen on Kongens Nytorv (*Map 3, B8, p253*) hosts mainly traditional ballet and opera, Stærkassen situated at Tordenskjoldsgade 5 (*Map 3, B8, p253*) has a varied repertoire of international and European drama, while the two performance spaces of the Turbinehallerne situated at Adelgade 10 (*Map 3, A8, p253*) stages 20 to 30 modern drama productions (mainly Danish) per season.

Det Ny Teater, Gammel Kongevej 29, **T** 33255075, www.detnyteater.dk   *Map 3, D1, p252* Elegant and grand theatre with three balconies and a capacity of 1,000. Mainstream productions, including international musicals such as Cats. Also stages modern ballet (see Dance, pXXX).

Edison, Edisonsvej 10, **T** 33211490, www.bettynansen.dk   *Map 2, C8, p251* Flexible theatre space (part of the Betty Nansen Teater) attracting good physical and experimental performances and new fringe drama.

Kaleidoskop, Nørrebrogade 37, **T** 35365302, www.kaleidoskop.dk   *Map 4, G2, p254* Modern experimental theatre and workshops. Venue for the acclaimed International Monologue Festival and other key events.

Østre Gasværk Teater, Nyborggade 17, **T** 39277177.   *Map 4, A6, p254* Old gasworks with a spectacular Dome. Stages a varied programme of modern and experimental performance art.

Terra Nova Teater, Vesterbro Kulturhus, Lyrskovgade 4, **T** 33799001, www.fast.dk/terranova   *Map 2, G10, p251* Experimental performances often around socio-political themes. Lots of international collaborations and often staged in English.

Copenhagen's most lively and enjoyable festivals are music-based ones, especially jazz, with a number of free events taking place at public venues around the city. It is worth visiting the Wonderful Copenhagen tourist office at the time of your visit to ask for specific information on current events and venues. The Summer Festival in Malmö also has a number of free events and a visit to the city is especially worthwhile when it is on.

Some festive events in Copenhagen, it has to be admitted, can verge on the side of tweeness, and the St Hans Eve Festival and the Queen's Birthday celebrations fall into this category.

April

Queen's birthday (16th) is celebrated at Amalienborg Slot. Queen Margrethe appears on the balcony at noon and waves to her subjects, with the royal guards prancing about the square in their full regalia.

Night Film Festival, see www.natfilm.dk, is a major film festival that finds its way into most of the city's cinemas.

May

May Day (1st) is celebrated across the city with colourful marches and brass bands threading their way from different starting points to a common destination in Fælled Park, where food, drink and music are the order of the day.

Copenhagen's Beer Festival (second weekend in May, 75kr) is a more serious (and sober) affair than you might expect. This is beer drinking as an art form and members Danish Beer Enthusiasts will teach you how to recognize that perfect brew. Big names like Carlsberg and Tuborg alongside British contributors like Greene King, Hall & Woodhouse, plus less familiar microbrews. There is no fixed venue and anyone interested in advance information should contact Stine Lolk at sl@tivoli.dk

Latin American Festival (date varies from year to year, T 33152002) is every bit as vibrant an affair as you would wish it to be. Music from Cuba and Brazil, lessons in salsa, samba and tango, food from the Caribbean and Latin America. Takes place in the city centre in the form of street parades with different bars and cafés. Well worth the 60kr admission.

Roskilde Festival

A few years ago, as many as 90,000 people would attend the Roskilde Festival, but then in 2000 came a tragedy when nine young men suffocated to death during a Pearl Jam concert.

For the 2002 concert, a maximum of 65,000 tickets, were on sale and they were all gone a week before the event started. The big bands appearing were hardly earth-shattering – Garbage, Red Hot Chilli Peppers, Chemical Brothers, Manu Chao – but what always makes Roskilde such a sell-out are the not-so-big names (2002 saw The Beta Band, Aimee Mann, Erikah Badu, Gotan Project) and local Danish talent. Well-organized and plenty of non-musical activities, including basketball courts, climbing walls, chill-out tent, and giant screens showing soccer. Check out the website (T 46366613, www.roskilde-festival.dk) for future festivals and booking.

June

Whitsun Carnival at Fælled Park, this time for a three-day, Latin-flavoured weekend bash with parades, floats and colourful costumes.

St Hans Eve Festival (23rd) celebrates the longest day of the year. The mid-summer festival, takes place on the northern beaches and in Fælled Park. Large bonfires are lit and the spirit of *hygee* prevails as Copenhageners frolic with the help of lager.

Roskilde Festival (over four days on the last weekend of the month) is the largest music festival in northern Europe and arguably the best on the continent (see Box above).

Hygee

Hygee, one of those words from another culture that defies exact translation, conjures up for Danes ideas of comfort and cosiness, a cheerful state of well-being. *Hygee* is essentially social in nature and usually carries very positive connotations, though for the disenchanted young Danish poet Michael Strunge (see p237) the concept becomes:

"The life-support machine of this comatose state...
Drip-fed with coffee and alcohol
the nation lies prostrate on a sterile bed
of obligatory friendliness."

July

The Jazz Festival (first Friday to the second Sunday in July, T 33932013, www.cjf.dk) takes over the city with over 600 concerts with the whole jazz repertoire being represented. The 2002 event brought Box of Toads, Doctor Structure, and Frederik Lundin Overdrive, and lots of free outdoor events. Ben Webster, Stan Getz and Dexter Gordon are just some of the American jazz players who settled in Copenhagen for short and long periods of time.

August

The Ballet Festival (last two weeks, T 39901500, www.xproduction.com) features international dancers and top performers from he Royal Danish Ballet.

Golden Days in Copenhagen (last two weeks, T 35421432, www.goldendays.dk) is a rich and varied celebration of early 19th-century Danish culture. The programme can be ordered on the website.

Images of Asia (takes place through August and September) is the 2003 focus of a cultural festival that annually celebrates the non-Western world (www.dccd.dk). Over 400 artists from Afghanistan to Mongolia and Japan enliven the city's stages.

October

Copenhagen's Gay and Lesbian Film Festival
(www.gayfilm.dk) takes place at the end of the month.

November

Autumn Jazz Festival (www.jazzfestival.dk) is another popular jazz event involving various pubs, clubs and entertainment centres hosting different musicians.

December

Christmas festivities, outside of the home, take the form of illuminations and decorations lighting up the city and creating scenes that you thought only existed on the covers of traditional Christmas cards. The artificial ice rink at Kongens Nytorv expresses the spirit that Danes just love about Christmas.

Shopping

Nørrebro is an up-and-coming shopping area for clothes, including second-hand gear. The streets to check out are Blågårdsgade and Elmegade. Antiques are found in this neighbourhood, too, mainly along Ravnsborggade. Back in the city centre, Vestergade, Studiestræde and Larsbjørnstræde are three streets near Rådhuspladsen that have lots of gratifying little record and second-hand clothes shops, far more interesting than most of the retail outlets on Strøget, though Illum Bolighus, Holmegaard, Royal Copenhagen and Georg Jensen at the top end of Strøget should not be missed. Købmagergade, running off Strøget, has lots of familiar names (French Connection, Diesel, etc) though far more enticing is Kronprinsensgarde home to some of Denmark's top fashion designers. Some of the best shops for gifts and small decorative items are to be found in the city's museums and art galleries. The most interesting shops are those retailing Danish and Swedish designs in home furniture, interior decoration and kitchen products.

Most shops open at 1000, closing around 1800 on weekdays (often a hour later on Fridays), 1600 or thereabouts on Saturdays, rarely open on Sundays. There are two good reasons for a shopping trip to Malmö (p118): the favourable exchange rate with sterling and the fact that most shops are open on Sundays.

Copenhagen

Antiques

Decor, Rømersgade 9, **T** 33148098. *Map 4, H4, p254* Vintage clothes, teddy bears and strange odds and ends pepper the stock. The shop always has a stall at the Saturday flea market across the road on Israels Plads (see below).

GB Antiques, Ved Glyptotek 6, **T** 21682529. *Map 3, E5, p252* Tucked away on a quiet street that runs by the side of Ny Carlsberg Glyptotek, this is the place for collectors of Royal Copenhagen pieces.

Veirhanen, Ravnsborggade 12, **T** 35353142, www.ravnsborggade.dk *Map 4, F3, p254* Almost chosen at random, *Veirhanen* is just one of more than 30 antique shops that line both sides of Ravnsborggade. *Veirhanen* has a neat collection of old suitcases, small furniture items, odds and ends and, like the other antique shops here, also opens on the first Sunday of each month.

Spunk & Co, Kompagnistræde 21, **T** 33127977, www.soelberg-antik.dk *Map 3, C6, p252* Alongside conventional antiques (but not Royal Copenhagen ceramics), this store is filled to overflowing with a dazzling array of art and artefacts, from original Russian icons to a 1940s German slot machine, South American indigenous crafts to vintage Star Wars items and military memorabilia.

Art

Basement, Knabrostræde 25, **T** 33149050. *Mon- Fri 1300-1800. Map 3, C6, p252* Contemporary art, mostly Danish, oil paintings from 1500-15,000kr, graphic art around 3,500kr. New artist every month; just up the road from *Spisehuset/La Bella Notte* restaurant.

Galloperiet, Christiania. *Mon- Fri 0930-1800. Map 3, C12, p253* To find this off-beat art gallery in Christiania, walk down Pusher Street a short distance and turn right into the street at Lorpen, a long building on the right with the Spiseloppen restaurant (p160) upstairs. Galloperietis further along, past the Loppen. Art exhibitions vary, usually original in one way or another, like the current collection of naive art that looks like the work of a Danish Rousseau.

Inuit, Kompagnistræde 21, **T** 33127977, www.soelberg-antik.dk *Map 3, C6, p252* Easy to find on the pedestrianized street south of and parallel to Strøget, this gallery of Eskimo art is a real one-off. Sculptures using reindeer antlers (from 650kr), carvings from the teeth of the walrus (3,000-5,000kr) and figurines from sperm whales from before they were protected. Next door, under the same management, the more eclectic Spunk & Co (above).

Books and maps

Nordisk Korthanel, Studiestræde 26-30, **T** 33382638. *Mon-Fri until 1730 and 1500 on Sat. Map 3, B4, p252* The best stock of travel guides and maps in the city.

Politikens Boghal, Rådhuspladsen 37, **T** 33472560. *Mon-Fri until 1900, 1600 on Sat. Map 3, C4, p252* The largest and best English-language bookshop in Copenhagen, with a good selection of fiction and non-fiction.

Window shopping
Be it brushes, blushers or other buys, Copenhagen has great shops.

Clothes and fashion

Bruuns Bazaar, Kronprinsengade 8, **T** 33321999,
www.bruunsbazaar.dk *Map 3, A7, p253* One of the prestigious,
trend-setting brand names that brought Scandinavian fashion
onto the pages of glossy lifestyle magazines.

Charlotte Sparre, Pistolstræde 4, **T** 33152315. *Map 3, A8,
p253* One of the better little boutiques in the streets behind
upper Strøget, *Charlotte Sparre* specializes in silk scarves,
200-350kr, and smart embroidered tops, sarongs and soft
leather trousers.

Donn ya Doll, Istedgade 55, **T** 33226635. *Map 3, F1, p252*
A tiny shop retailing club gear, shoes, clothes, clocks and gizmos.

Guns & Gents, Skindergade 31, **T** 33912424. *Map 3, B6, p252*
Fashionable dress for the outdoor life as well as fishing and
shooting gear; good selection of outdoor jackets and shirts from
Sweden and South Shields.

Hallgren, Købmagergade 39, **T** 33381500. *Map 3, B7, p252*
Two floors of shoes and unisex, Danish-designed Jaco Form and
Trim brands on the ground floor. Expect to pay around 800kr.

Ichinen, Istedgade 59, **T** 33794717. *Map 3, F1, p252* A small shop,
retailing some wild-looking T-shirts and other clothes, typical of
the new kind of low-key boutique beginning to appear along this
stretch of Istedgade.

KiKi, Blågårdsgade 29, **T** 35340060. *Map 4, G2, p254* Silk dresses,
around 390kr, raw silk scarves around 250kr, and crockery – all
from Vietnam in a shop owned by a Buddhist monk and with
profits going to a children's hospital.

Klædebo, Blågårdsgade 3, **T** 35360227. *Mon-Fri 1200-1800, Sat
1030-1400. Map 4, G2, p254* Former cellar cheese shop featuring
the work of four designers, two of whom specialize in children's
clothes, with skirts, tops and dresses all around 400-600kr.

Munth plus Simonsen, Kronprinsengade 11, **T** 3320312. *Map 4,
A7, p255* Vying with Bruuns Bazaar for top-notch designer-wear in
the city, debuting at the 2000 pret-à-porter fashion week in Paris
and now selling around the world.

Naturlivis, Blågårdsgade 17, **T** 35343757. *Mon-Fri opens at noon,
Sat at 1000. Map 4, G2, p254* T-shirts, trousers (around 650kr),
alpaca socks, using mostly hemp.

Storm, Store Regnegade 1, **T** 33930014. *Map 4, A7, p255* Hot fashion for both sexes in a very design-conscious store, hence the white glare of neon, glass cabinets and oh-so-cool changing room. Danish brands like Daughters of Style and Tine Jensen, Baum & Pferdgarten alongside a flurry of foreign designers.

Y's - Yohji Yamamoto, Gammel Mønt 10, **T** 33930602. *Map 3, A7, p255* Japanese designer Yamamoto's first Nordic boutique, designed by architects at Henning Larsen's firm, is white indeed. Classical, timeless styles, with pure wool suits for women around 2,500kr and more affordable silk and cotton clothes, shoes, handbags, scarves, and the designer's own perfume brand (325kr).

Second-hand clothes

Kirkens Genbrug, Blågårdsgade 39. *Map 4, G2, p254* Shirts, tops, jackets, in good condition and ready to wear, for men and women.

Kbh K, Studiestræde 32B, **T** 33330360. *Mon-Fri 1100-1900, Sat 1100-1600. Map 3, B4, p252* Not the only such store on and around Studiestræde but one with the largest stock of shirts, tops, trousers, dresses, leather coats, bags and caps. Zippy changing rooms and some decorative items too. Located in a courtyard next to the yellow-painted *Dubrovnik* restaurant.

UFF, Vestergade 14, **T** 33323431. *Map 3, C5, p252* Men's section on the right, mostly leather and suede jackets around 360kr, department-sized women's section at the back.

Department stores

Illum, Østergade 52, **T** 33144002. *Map 3, B7, p253* Start on the lower floors and work your way up from the food and cosmetics to clothes, fashion, household goods and the airy café and restaurant under a glass roof at the top.

Magasin du Nord, Kongens Nytorv 13, **T** 33114433. *Map 3, B8, p253* Opposite the Royal Theatre and with an equally grand façade, *Magasin du Nord* has six floors of consumer goodies as well as an excellent foodstore and Lego-dominated toy department.

Design

AA Audio, Gothersgade 58, **T** 33141453. *Map 4, H6, p254* A hi-fi store that specializes in classic merchandise, like Jacob Jensen's designs for *Bang og Olufsen* over 30 years ago, old gramophones and transistor radios, restoring the stuff if necessary.

Bang og Olufsen, Østergade 35, **T** 33150422. *Map 3, B8, p253* You know the reputation, now view the source of the ultimate in ultra-sleek, minimalist hi-fi. Prices are competitive and worth comparing with what you would pay at home for the same models.

Casa Shop, Store Regnegade 2, **T** 32327041. *Map 3, A7, p253* Easy to find, just follow Kronprinsensgade off Købmagergade from Strøget, this is the place for leading designs in home furniture. Shipping can be arranged, but many of the products are portable.

Designer's Shop, Gråbrødretorv 3, **T** 33930104. *Map 3, B6, p253* Close by the *Pedar Oxe* restaurant (p143), jugs, watches, cutlery and table top items by Nicolas Nicolaou, originally from Cyprus but resident in Copenhagen for a quarter of a century.

Georg Jensen, Amagertorv 4, **T** 33114080, www.royalshopping.dk *Map 3, B6, p252* Jensen opened his workshop in 1904 and continues to turn out fine silverware. The

White lines
Simple shapes characterize much of Danish design and style.

ground floor has jewellery, watches and sophisticated pieces from modern designers, upstairs are silverware and cutlery.

Gubi, Grønnegade 10, **T** 33326368. *Map 3, A8, p253* Snazzy lamps and other lifestyle yokes for the home amidst larger items of domestic furniture (shipping can be arranged) in this highly-regarded design-conscious store. Come here for ideas, not purchases.

Holmegaard, Amagertorv 8, **T** 33124477, www.royalshopping.dk *Map 3, B6, p252* Scandinavian and Italian glass of the highest quality and with a sufficiently wide range of products and prices to suit most budgets.

Illum Bolighus, Amagertorv 11, **T** 33141941, www.royalshopping.dk   *Map 3, B6, p252*   Making *Habitat* look like second-hand chintz, this is where Copenhageners shop for wedding presents meant to impress, or when buying something special for their own homes. Kitchenware, Georg Jensen clocks, Kosta Boda coloured glassware, bedclothes, stationery, shoes, duvets, dressing gowns, lighting, watches, furniture, gizmos, and not just Danish designs.

Rosenthal Studio-Haus, Frederiksberggade 21, **T** 33142101, www.rosenthal.dk   *Map 3, C5, 252*   On the right as you begin walking up Lower Strøget from Rådhuspladsen, Rosenthal Studio-Haus features contemporary and avant-garde designs. A Philippe Starck door stopper at 15,500kr might seem over the top, but the Jensen cutlery, Michael Graves kitchen tools, Bulgari tableware, and glass by Swedish designer Bertil Vallien are lovely, if costly, to behold.

Royal Copenhagen, Amagertorv 6, **T** 33137181, www.royalshopping.dk   *Map 3, B6, p252*   Hand-painted figurines, Blue Fluted cups and vases (it takes 1,197 brushstrokes to decorate a single dinner plate of the Blue Fluted service designed in 1775), Flora Danica dinner service, humble coffee mugs. From 200kr to astronomical amounts. Also a shop at the factory (see p76).

Erotica

Fetish Fashion, Gasværksvej 4, **T** 33253371.   *Mon-Fri 1300-1800, Sat 1100-1500.   Map 3, E1, p252*   A tiny store specializing in boots and suits.

Lust, Mikkel Bryggersgade 3A, **T** 33330110, www.lust.dk   *Map 3, C5, p252*   A decidedly superior and sleazeless sex shop, take the first turning on the right when walking up Strøget from

Rådhuspladsen, with three small levels devoted to edible undies and other lingerie, sex aids, an erotic version of ginseng and other promising concoctions in bottles.

Plan E, Istedgade 30, **T** 33219930. *Map 3, E2, p252* There are a few sex shops along Istedgade, but most are not set out in the supermarket style of Plan E, on the corner with Viktoriagade. A wide range of stimulators, some kooky male and female mannequin kits, sex toys and aids, videos and magazines. The *Copenhagen Gay Centre Shop* is a few doors up, while back towards the railway station, close to the *Centrum Hotel*, there is the *Delta Love Store* and, next door, the infelicitously-named but very pleasant *Spunk Bar*, is a good watering hole.

SM Shop, Studiostræde 12, **T** 33127912. *Mon-Fri from 1100, closing 1400 on Sat. Map 3, B5, p252* Regular sex toys and lingerie, but the specialty is bondage gear with a nice line in English corsets, plus floggers and whips, equipment and magazines.

Markets

Israel Plads. *May-Oct, Mon-Sat 0800-1700 fruit and vegetables, Sat 0800-1700 bric-a-brac. Map 4, H4, p252* A short walk from Nørre- port station, the Saturday flea market is a lively affair with many of the city's antique traders setting up stalls and performing a more downmarket role than usual. No absolute bargains, but can be fun.

Music

Accord, Vestergade 37, **T** 33150039, www.accord.dk *Map 3, C5, p252* Rock, reggae, jazz, dance, soul-funk, hip hop, punk/ska, indie, classical, Danish rock and jazz. Second-hand music is available in their smaller store around the corner on Larsbjørnsstrade.

Baden Baden, Larsbjørnsstrade 15, **T** 33154030. *Map 3, C5, p252*
   On the corner with Studiestræde, a fair selection of vinyl releases from indie and dance genres, a bit of hip hop; useful place to spot flyers for up-and-coming music events.

Street Dance Records, Vestergade 17, **T** 33159070, www.streetdance.com *Mon-Fri 1100-1800, Sat 1100-1600. Map 3, C5, p252* House, hip hop and electronic, with some bargains to be found among the old vinyl and CD releases downstairs.

The Other Music, Kronprinsensgade 7, **T** 33937493, www.theothermusic.com *Map 3, A7, p253* Avant-garde vinyl and CD music, trance, downbeat, drum 'n' bass. This is the place to find the best of modern Danish music, like Morten Skovgaard Danielsen.

Miscellaneous

Czar, Købmagergade 32, **T** 33129403. *Map 3, B7, p253*
Pedestrianized Købmagergadeclothes has too many brand-name stores for its own good and this makes *Czar*, a cheese shop, even more of a delightful find. The open front is an invitation to wander in and with over 400 Danish cheeses (and non-Danish ones) attractively displayed, you may want to find room in your luggage for a kilo or two.

Hemp House, Larsbjørnstraede 22, **T** 33914171, www.hemp house.dk *Mon-Fri 1200-1730, Sat 1100-1500. Map 3, B5, p252*
On Larsbjørnstraede, the second turning on the left when walking up Vestergade from Rådhuspladsen, everything in the shop is made from hemp: trousers, shirts, bags, soap, body lotion, plus seeds of course.

Pusher Street, Christiania. *Daily 0900-2200. Map 3, C12, p253*
See also p90 Christiania's busiest street is laid out with stalls

selling cannabis, in blocks or joints, bags of skunk, pipes, pipe fittings (attached to Carlsberg bottles and other memorabilia), pamphlets of cannabis recipes, books on growing the plant, skunk seeds from Holland – all clearly priced and weighing scales at the ready. Expect to pay around 100kr for five ready-rolled joints and a similar price for three of the skunk-filled version. Cannabis prices start at about 40kr a gram, with discounts for larger quantities, higher quality stuff from Morocco (the country of origin is usually specified) is about twice this price. Skunk seeds, imported from Holland and sold in packets of half a dozen seeds, range in price from 120kr to over 1,000kr for the top-notch, super-charged variety.

Around Copenhagen

Louisiana Shop, Gammel Strandvej, Humlebæk. **T** 49190791, www.louisiana.dk *Mon-Tue, Thu-Sun 1000-1700, Wed 1000-2200.* The shop at the famed Louisiana, p101, aspiring to department-store status, is filled with much more than just art books, postcards and posters. Strong on kitchenware, including sets of designer cutlery, hip stationery, a designer bicycle for 8,000kr, even the sets of garden tools fit the unifying theme of quality Danish-designed goods.

Viking Ship Museum Shop, Vindebode 12, Roskilde, **T** 46300200, www.vikingeskibsmuseet.dk *May-Sep 0900-1700, Oct-Apr 1000-1600.* Mostly quality merchandise with a Viking theme, including books, jigsaws, models, mobiles, knives, glass items and some fashionable scarves.

David Design, Stortorget 25, Malmö, **T** (040) 300000, www.david.se *Mon-Fri 1000-1800, Sat 1000-1500, Sun 1200-1600.* Home items from the David Design collection as well as from other leading Scandinavian designers in this centrally located shop in the city's main square.

Form & Design Centre, Lilla Torg, Malmö, **T** (040) 6645150. *Mon-Fri 1000-1800, Sat 1000-1500, Sun 1200-1600*. There is usually an exhibition of some kind or other in the field of design or architecture, while upstairs there is a smart café where you can read design magazines and, on the top floor, a shop selling Scandinavian designs in glass, textiles and kitchen accessories.

Danes love soccer and the city has two professional clubs, Brøndby and FC København, that play throughout the year apart from a winter break covering December to mid-March. The two clubs are currently locked into a championship battle and if they are playing each other there is no chance of buying a ticket on the day. Every Sunday throughout July and August, football enthusiasts from Copenhagen and all over Europe compete in the Unity Cup at Fælled Park (see p89). Individuals and teams wishing to enter can show up on a Sunday or telephone (T 33224543) for further information.

Copenhagen has excellent sport facilities which visitors can avail themselves of and it takes little more than a phone call to confirm details. Jogging is very safe and very popular in the public parks and you are unlikely to find yourself the sole runner. Many of the better hotels have first-class sport and fitness facilities and the DGI-byens (see p129) excels in this respect.

Copenhagen

Golf

Copenhagen Golf Course, T 39630483. *Reached by a train to Klampenborg and then bus no 388. Map 5, p256* Eighteen-hole course. The green fees are about 300kr plus the hire of equipment at around 200kr.

Copenhagen Indoor Golf Centre, Refshalevej 177B, Christianshavn, T 32544332. *Open mid-Sep-mid-Oct, Mon-Fri 1600-2100, Sat and Sun 1200-1700; mid-Oct-Apr, Mon and Fri 1100-2100, Tue to Thu 1100-2200, Sat and Sun 0900-1900.* Reached by bus no 8. *Map 3, C10, p253* The cost of using these facilities is around 125kr an hour.

Gyms and fitness centres

The sports centre, *DGI-byen hotel*, near Central Station on Tietgensgade, T 33298090, www.dgibyen.dk *Map 3, E4, p252* Fitness centre with sauna, steam bath and climbing wall.

Vesterbro Fitness Centre, Angelsgade 4, T 33220500. Reached by train to Enghave or by bus nos 3, 10, 16, 650S. *Map 5, p256* It is less expensive than the *DGI-byen hotel* centre, at around 60-100kr.

Scala Form and Fitness, Vesterbrogade 2E, T 33321002. *Map 3, D2, p252* Similarly priced as Vesterbro.

Football

Brøndby, Vester Boulevard, T 43630810, www.brondby-if.dk *Reached by taking the S-Tog to Glostrup and then bus no 131. Map 5,*

Sports

p256 Brøndby's own stadium. Tickets are about 100kr and they play on Saturday, Sunday or Monday afternoons.

FC København, Parken stadium, **T** 35437400, www.fck.dk *Reached by train to Østerport and bus no 1.* FC København was hatched in 1992 and, lacking the working-class origins of Brøndby, are derided by supporters of their rivals as a bunch of yuppies. Tickets are about 100kr. Play on Saturday, Sunday or Monday afternoons.

Swimming

Sports centre, adjoining the *DGI-byen* hotel near Central Station on Tietgensgade, **T** 33298090, www.dgibyen.dk *Mon-Thu 0630-2100, Fri 0630-1900, Sat and Sun 0900-1700. Map 3, E4, p256* It has a pool designed to avoid the usual, competitively-minded swimming lanes, and it is lovely to use outside of weekends when children and their families colonize the place. There was also a sauna, steam rooms, plunge pool and other facilities.

Vesterbro, Angelsgade 4, **T** 33220500. *Mon 1000-2100, Tue and Thu 0700-1700, Wed 0700-1900, Fri 0700-1600, Sat 0900-1400. 25kr. Reached by train to Enghave or by bus nos 3, 10, 16, 650S.* This is a city council-run pool, which is less expensive than the sports centres.

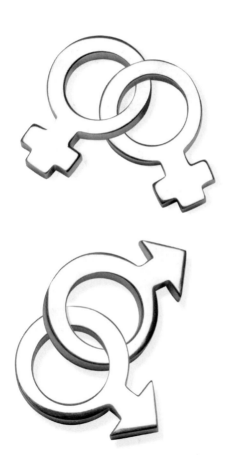

Gay Denmark is progressive and liberal. They were the first country in the world to recognise same-sex marriages back in 1989, and in 1999 it became possible for married same-sex couples to adopt the children of their partners.

In terms of the Copenhagen gay scene, it is very small. This is a product of the Danish population being gay-friendly and most bars and club being very mixed. There are however, still a number of bars, cafés and events that cater exclusively for gay clientele and positively signal gay visibility. What the scene lacks in size, it very makes up for with charm.

Radio Rosa (FM 91.4) is a popular gay radio station that broadcasts in Danish, and HC Ørsteds Park is a favourite well-known cruising ground for the gay population (it's littered with 'bird boxes' dispensing condoms).

Bars and cafés

Can Can, Mikkel Bryggrsgade 11. *1600-0200. Map 3, C5, p252*
Juke box music and drag queens.

Centralhjørnet, Kattesundet 18. *1200-0100. Map 3, C5, p252*
Oldest gay bar in the city, still packing in an older leather-clad
crowd.

Jailhouse Copenhagen, Studiostræde 12, T 33152255.
1200-0200. Map 3, B5, p252 Only jail-bar in the city, bartenders in
uniform serving drinks and food.

Heaven Café, Bar & Restaurant, Kompagnistræde 18, T 33151900,
www.heaven-copenhagen.dk *1100-0200. Map 3, C6, p252* Laid
back pre-clubbing bar with party crowd and happy hours called
'Heavenly Hours'.

Oscar Bar & Café, Rådhuspladsen 87, T 33120999,
www.oscarbarcafe.dk *1200-0200 (food until 2200). Map 3, C4, p252*
A new café and bar, centrally located by the town hall.

Never Mind, Nørre Voldgade. *1000-0600. Map 3, A4, p252*
Situated close to the HC Ørsteds Park. Kitsch and popular with
'older' men. Open late.

Cozy Bar, Studiostræde 24, www.cosybar.dk *Mon-Wed, Sun
2400-0600, Thu-Sat 1100-0700. Map 3, B4, p252* One of the oldest
gay bars in the city. Very cruisey and debauched with a mixed
up-for-it crowd. Happy hour 2200-0200. Open late.

Discos

Pan Disco, Knabrostræde 3, www.pan-cph.dk *Map 3, B6, p252*
A pink triangle sign on the street outside a former warehouse, with techno on the ground floor, Marlene Dietrich lounge upstairs and camp classic pop on the top floor.

Catwalk, Kattesundet 4. Weekend-only danceclub plus a relaxed bar which opens daily. Mixed crowd.

Festivals and events

Torch-lit procession (last Sunday in May) is an annual event held in memory of those who have died of AIDS.

MrGay.dk Beauty Competition (June), www.mrgay.dk

Miss World Goes Gay (August 2004) sees the biennial beauty contest for drag queens.

Gay Pride Parade (mid-August) is the annual parade known locally as Mermaid Pride with a 1,000 or so gays and lesbians lighting up the streets with floats and 'dykes on bikes', www.mermaidpride.dk

Gay and lesbian film festival (October).

Choral works are performances by one of Copenhagen's gay choirs – Carmen Curlers (www.carmencurlers.dk), Schwanzen Sänger Knaben (www.schwanzen.dk), The Boy's Choir (www.drenge koret.dk) and The Women's Choir (www.kvindekoret.dk). Keep an eye open throughout the year.

Organizations and information

The National Association for Gays and Lesbians (LBL), Teglgårdstræd 13, T33131948, www.ibl.dk *Map 3, B4, p252* It was founded in 1948 as the first of its kind. Its office has books and current information that visitors can check out and a gay guide to Copenhagen is downloadable from the web site. Another useful website is www.copenhagen-gay-life.dk

Sleeping

C **Carsten's Guest House**, 5th floor, Christians Brygge 28, T33149107. *Map 4, D8, p253* Ring the door bell labelled Carsten Appel. Small rooms but lovely roof garden and kitchen for use by guests.

C **Copenhagen Rainbow**, Frederiksberggade 25C, T33141020, www.copenhagen-rainbo.dk *Map 3, E3, p252* Centrally located, close to Central Station, a range of room types and free internet access.

E **Hotel Windsor**, Frederiksborggade 30, T33110830, F33116387, www.hotelwindsor.dk *Map 3, H4, p252* Well-established gay hotel, beginning to show its age but friendly and a range of single, double and triple rooms.

With space reserved on trains and buses for pushchairs and prams, terrific children's sections in museums and galleries and lots else to see and do, taking young children to Copenhagen can be a breeze – though older teenagers might find the pace too civilized at times. Even the Jazz Festival (see p191) has a special programme on 'jazz for children'. Don't forget, too, that children's bikes can be hired (see p224) and safely used. There are kids' menus in most restaurants, and special seats for toddlers are usually available on request.

The beaches (see p102) are a big draw for young children and there are a number of other attractions north of the city. Louisiana (see p101) is all geared up for family visits, with special strollers and carrying slings for transporting the very young available. A special Children's Wing and the Lake Garden is open with child-friendly instalments during the day. If visiting Akvarium (see p103) check the feeding times and touch pool times. The Experimentarium (see p107) with its crazy mirrors, computer rooms and logic puzzles will amuse older children.

Museums

Nationalmuseet, Ny Vestergade 10, **T** 33693369, www.natmus.dk
Tue-Sun 1000-1700. Adults 40kr, children free. Free Wed. Buses 1, 2, 5,
6, 8, 10, 28-30, 32, 33, 550S, 650S. Map 3, D6, p252 See also p44
The children's section in the National Museum includes an entire
school room from the early 20th century ("In the good old days it
was tough on the Head/getting heart attacks as he whacked
away", reads a poem by Thorstein Thomsen) and, in room 301,
there are lots of Egyptian mummies.

Statens Museum for Kunst, Sølvgade 48, **T** 33748494,
www.smk.dk *Tue-Sun 1000-1700, Wed 1000-2000, closed on public*
holidays, Easter Mon, Whit Mon, 23-5 Dec, 30 Dec-1 Jan. Adults 50kr.
Free Wed. Buses 10, 14, 40, 42, 43, 184, 185, 150S, 72E, 79E, 173E.
S-Tog Østerport, Nørreport. Metro, Nørreport. Map 4, G7, p255 See
also p80 The children's section of the Statens Museum for Kunst
features exhibitions of original art suitable for children aged 6-12
and there is also a workshop for hands-on expression. During the
summer holidays (24 June-4 August), special workshop activities
take place on afternoons between Tuesday and Friday (20kr per
child). The gallery's bookshop has a section of art books suitable for
children, and a kids' table with crayons and paper.

Zoologisk Have, Roskildevej 32, **T** 72200200, www.zoo.dk *Map*
2, E5, p250 As zoos go, Copenhagen's attempt to offer animals a
semblance of their natural environment is laudable enough. The
children's section has a hands-on approach and urban youngsters
will love it.

Zoologisk Museum, Universitetsparken 15, **T** 35321001,
www.zoologiskmuseum.dk *Tue-Sun 1100-1700. Adults 25kr,*
children 10kr. Buses 18, 24, 43, 150S, 184, 185. Map 4, A2, p254
See also p78 Charts the zoological history from 20,000 years ago

Kids

to the present day in an entertaining way. It is a great museum for children.

Child minding services

HH-Babysitting, **T** 70208151, www.hh-baby.dk Available daily from 0900 to 2200. The hourly rate is 40kr, plus an agency fee of 40kr and any public transport costs for the sitter.

Museums

Orlogsmuseet, Overgaden Oven Vandet 58, **T** 32546363, www.orlogsmuseet.dk *Tue-Sun 1200-1600. Adults 30kr, children 20kr. Buses 2, 8, 9, 28, 31, 37, 350S. Map 3, D10, p253 See also p92* The Royal Danish Naval Museum has a children's section complete with a gun deck, a submarine replica to clamber aboard in the main museum and, with a picnic area downstairs, an opportunity to feed the family.

Viking Ship Museum, Vindeboder 12, Roskilde,**T** 46300200, www.vinkingeskibsmuseet.dk *May-Sep 0900-1700, Oct-Apr 1000-1600. Adults 60kr in summer, 45kr in winter, children 35/28kr. Train to Roskilde and a 20-min walk or bus 216 or 605 from the station. Map 5, p256 See also p114* This museum has a children's section with two Viking ship models to clamber aboard, a warship and a trader, plus a selection of copies of artefacts like warriors' and sailors' clothes, weapons, commodities and jewellery. During the summer there are also craftwork activities such as painting, making hand-made lime bark bracelets and sewing leather purses.

Tycho Brahe Planetarium, Gammel Kongevej 10, **T** 33121224, www.tycho.dk *Mon, Fri-Sun 1030-2100, Tue and Thu 0930-2100, Wed 0945-2100. Adults 85kr, children 65kr. Buses 1, 14, 16. Map 3, D2, p252 See also p74* There are films on topics like dolphins and ancient Egypt that are suitable for children aged 4 and up, while the Cosmic Voyage film is for 7 and up. Kids might pester you for purchases of framed holograms or hologram watches and other jazzy merchandise in the shop.

The Guinness World of Records Museum, Østergade 16, T 33323131, www.guinness.dk *Jun-Aug 1000-2230, Sep-May, Mon-Thu 1000-1800, Fri-Sat 1000-2000. Adults 74kr, children 27kr. Map 3, B8, p253* Five hundred of the world's record breaking achievements on show.

Ripley's Believe it or Not Museum, Rådhuspladsen, T 33918991, www.ripleys.dk *Jan-Mar 1000-1800, Jun-Aug 0930-2230, Sep-Dec Mon-Thu and Sun 1000-1800, Fri-Sat 1000-2000. Adults 74kr, children 57kr. Buses 2, 6, 8, 14, 16, 28-30, 32, 33, 67-69,173E, 250S. Map 3, C5, p252 See also p37* The world in miniature. Exhibits recording weird and wonderful phenomena.

Parks

Tivoli and Bakken amusement parks The fact that the rides at Tivoli (p35) are not exactly sphincter-tightening makes them ideal for young children but disappointing for older kids who might prefer the Bakken amusement park (p).

Fælled Park *Map 4, B4, p254 See also p89* Has playgrounds and an open-air swimming pool. A good place to head for for a short break from the city.

Amalienborg *Map 4, H10, p255 See also p65* The changing of the guard at Amalienborg and a canal boat trip are two ideas for a family outing.

Restaurants

Jensen's Bøfhus, Gråbrødretorv 15, T33327800. *Mon-Thu, Sun 1100-2230, Fri-Sat 1100-2330. Map 3, B6, p252 See also p143*
This is especially suitable for family dining.

Base Camp, Halvtolv Bygningen 148, **T** 70232318. *Wed-Thu 1800-0100, Fri-Sat 1100-1700. Closed on Mon and Thu between Oct-May. Bus no 8 stops close by this huge eatery that seats up to 600. Map 3, F12, p253 See also p160* Base Camp has a play room and space for children to wander around in safely.

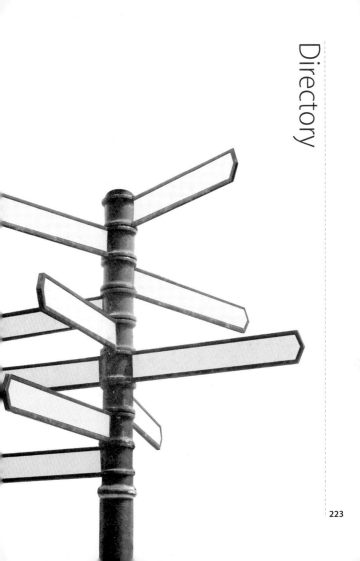

Directory

Airline offices

Air Canada, Vester Farimagsgade 1, **T** 33114555. **British Airways**, Rådhuspladsen 16, **T** 80208020. **British Midland**, Hammerichsgade 1, **T** 70102000. **Maersk Air**, Rådhuspladsen 16, **T** 33146000. **Scandinavian Airlines**, *Radisson SAS Royal Hotel*, **T** 70102000.

Banks and ATMs

Banks open 0930 to 1600 or 1700 on weekdays, some closing 1800 on Thursday. ATMs are outside most of them and major credit cards are accepted. Exchange bureaux are dotted about town, including Central Station and at Vesterbrogade 28.

Bicycle hire

Expect to pay around 50kr a day, 125kr for 3 days, with a deposit of around 300kr. There are also the free bikes (p26). **Københavns Cykler**, Central Station, **T** 33338613. *Mon-Fri 0800-1800, Sat 0900-1300. Jul and Aug, Sun 1000-1300.* **Tandems**, children's bikes and trailers also available. **Københavns Cyklebørs**, Gothersgade 157, **T** 33140717. **Dan Wheel**, Colbjørnsensgade 3, Vesterbro, **T** 31871423. **Cykelkliniken**, **T** 6116666, on Carlsgarten, which is directly behind the railway station. From 75sek a day.

Car hire

Rack rates for companies like **Avis** are from 500kr for a small car for 2 to 6 days. **Avis**, Kampmannsgade 1, **T** 33734099, www.avis.com Airport, **T** 32512299. **Budget**, Helgolandsgade 2, **T** 33557000. Airport, **T** 32523900.

Credit card lines

Visa, **Mastercard**, **Access**, **T** 44892500. **American Express**, **T** 80010021.

Dentists
For emergencies, **Tandlægevagten**, Oslo Plads 14, **T** 35380251. *Weekdays 0800-2100, weekends 1000-1400*. Payment by cash.

Disabled
Facilities for the disabled are generally excellent and the Wonderful Copenhagen tourist office (p) dispenses a list of useful information. Trains are wheel-chair accessible.

Doctors
EU residents receive free treatment; UK nationals should carry form E111, available from UK post offices, and use it to claim refund for medicines and doctors' fees from a local health insurance office (the tourist office will provide addresses). For a doctor, weekdays 0800-1600, **T** 33154600; evenings and weekends, **T** 70130041. Expect to pay 400-600kr. See also Hospitals and Pharmacies above.

Electricity
The supply is 220-240V, 50Hz AC, as in Britain, and sockets generally require a 2-pin plug, so a continental adapter may be necessary. North American equipment requires a transformer.

Embassies
Australia, Strandboulevarden 122, **T** 39292077. **Canada**, Kristen Bernikowsgade, **T** 33483200. **Ireland**, Østbanegade 21, **T** 35423233. **UK**, Kastelsvej 40, **T** 35445200. **USA**, Dag Hammerskjölds Allé 24, **T** 35553144.

Emergency numbers
T 112 for the emergency services.

Directory

Hospitals

24-hr emergency departments are at: **Amager Hospital**, Kastrupvej 63, **T** 32343234. Bus no 9. **Frederiksberg Hospital**, Nordre Fasanvej 57, Frederiksberg, **T** 38163816. Bus nos 2, 11, 29, 39, 100. See also Doctors and Dentists above and Pharmacies below.

Internet/email

Most hotels and hostels have online computers for use by guests, usually free in hotels. **Boomtown Netcafé** is near Central Station and Tivoli at Axeltorv, **T** 33321032. **NetPoint**, at the *Radisson SAS Royal Hotel* (p127), **T** 70221008. **Delmonet Café**, Blågårdsgade 4, is one of the cheapest you'll find at 10kr for half an hour. *1300-2400*.

Left luggage

Left luggage facilities at the airport and Central Station.

Libraries

Hovedbiblioteket, Krystalgade 15, is the main city library and stocks some English-language publications. *Mon-Fri 1000-1900, Sat 1000-1400.*

Lost property

Contact the police office at Slotsherrensvej 113, Vanløse, **T** 38745261. For items left on a bus, **T** 36131415 and then 1; on a train, **T** 33162110.

Media

English-language newspapers and magazines are sold at some outlets in Central Station and along Strøget. For *Copenhagen Post*, see p30. Radio news in English, Mon-Fri at 0840 and 1100, 1710 and 2200, on Radio Denmark International, medium wave 1062 Mhz. BBC Radio 4 can be picked up on long wave 198 Mhz.

Pharmacies (late night)
Steno Apotek, Vesterbrogade 6C, **T** 33148266 (24 hours).
Sønerbro Apotek, **Amagerbrogade**, **T** 32580140. See also
Doctors and Hospitals and above.

Police
For emergencies, **T** 112. Otherwise, **T** 33141448 and ask for details
of the station nearest to you. There is a police post in **Central
Station**, **T** 33153801, and the airport, **T** 32451448, and the one
nearest to the hotel area in Vesterbro is at Halmtorvet 20,
T 33251448.

Post offices

For inquiries, **T** 33415600. The main post office, and main post restante depot is at Tietgensgade 35, *Mon-Fri 1100-1800, Sat 1000-1300*. The post office in Central Station, *Mon-Fri 0800-2100, Sat 0900-1600, Sun 1000-1600*. Letters and postcards to other parts of Europe are 6kr.

Public holidays

The changeable dates are those for 2002. **New Year's Day** (1 Jan), **Maundy Thursday**, **Good Friday**, **Easter Sunday**, **Easter Monday**, **Great Prayer Day** (26 Apr), **Ascension Day**, **Whitsun**, **Constitution Day** (5 Jun), **Christmas Eve** (24 Dec), **Christmas Day** (25 Dec), **Boxing Day** (26 Dec), **New Year's Eve** (31 Dec).

Religious services

International Church of Copenhagen, Vartov Church, Favergade 27, **T** 39624785. Weekly Sunday service, 1130.
Sakrementskirken, Nørrebrogade 27, **T** 44947678. Roman Catholic service on Sunday at 1800.

Student organizations

USE IT, Rådhuspladsen 13, **T** 33730620, www.useit.kk.dk *Mon-Wed 1100-1600, Thu 1100-1800, Fri 1100-1400*. A youth information office.

Taxi

Taxis can be hailed in the street, look for a light on the roof of the vehicle that indicates it is available for hire. **Københavns Taxi**, **T** 35353535, **Hovedstadens Taxi**, **T** 38777777 and, for minibuses, **Dams Service**, **T** 32952221. **Quickshaws**, **T** 70201375, offer bike taxis.

Telephone
Public telephones, taking phone cards or coins, are to be found everywhere. All coins of 10kr and above are accepted, while the phone cards of 30kr, 50kr and 100kr are more convenient for longer calls including international ones. They can be purchased at post offices and kiosks at train stations. Denmark's dialling code is 45. Dial 113 for international directory inquiries and 118 for domestic inquiries.

Time
It is 1 hr ahead of GMT/UTC. Clocks moved forward 1 hr for summer time, from the last Sun in Mar to the last Sun in Oct. *Klokken* is Danish for o'clock and appears as kl in schedules.

Tipping
A service charge is nearly always included in bills for meals, hotel costs and taxi fares and tipping on this is not generally expected. Rounding up a bill for a small amount is not uncommon.

Toilets
Public toilets, normally free, are found at train stations and large shops. Showers are available at Central Station and the airport.

Transport inquiries
For bus queries, **T** 36131415, www.ht.dk   For S-Tog trains, **T** 33141701, www.s-tog.dk   See also below.

Train
Copenhagen's Central Station, **T** 33141701, www.dsb.dk   For regular trains, **T** 70131415. For international train travel, **T** 70131416.

A sprint through history

4000 BC	Earliest evidence of a settlement in what is now Copenhagen.
AD 1043	First written reference to the small fishing village of Havn. See Viking history, p236.
1167	Bishop Absalon built a castle on the island (Slotsholmen) opposite facing Havn.
1250	København (Merchants Haven) became a walled market town.
1417	A new castle was built and Copenhagen's prosperity grew as the Sound Toll was imposed on all vessels passing through the Øresund, the channel of water dividing Denmark from Sweden.
1443	Copenhagen replaced Roskilde as the capital.
1588	Christian IV became king and rebuilt parts of his capital.
1746	Frederik V became king and during his reign the present-day shape of Copenhagen was laid down. Large rebuilding projects after a major fire in 1795.
1807	The British sent a fleet under Nelson to Copenhagen to exert control in the Napoleonic Wars (1796-1815) against revolutionary France. The city was bombarded and the Danish fleet destroyed.
1830	The beginning of Denmark's Golden Age and a cultural renaissance associated with the disparate achievements of figures like Hans Christian Andersen, the philosopher Kierkegaard, and the sculptor Thorvaldsen.

1850	The beginning of the industrial age and the development of workers' areas in Vesterbro and Nørrebro.
1940	Denmark invaded by Nazi Germany and resistance gradually hardened to armed resistance.
1943	In response to Nazi plans to round up and deport Denmark's Jews, the resistance movement was able to mobilize citizens' willingness to help. Over 90% of the Jews were smuggled to safety in Sweden.
1950s	The beginning of an ambitious social welfare programme for the whole of Danish society.
1960s	Boom years for the Danish economy and immigrants invited to take up the kind of poorly-paid jobs that Copenhageners were turning their noses up at.
1971	Disused army barracks on Christianshavn taken over by squatters and the beginning of the 'free City' of Christiania.
1992	Denmark wins the soccer European Championships and the team appears on a balcony of Rådhuspladsen.
2000	The Øresund Bridge, a road and rail link opened between Copenhagen and Malmö in Sweden.
2001	Elections brought the far right into a government and anti-immigration laws follow.
2003	Denmark, a stalwart member state of the EU, continues to remain outside the euro zone. As with Britain it seems only a matter of time before Denmark adopts the European currency.

Art and architecture

12th century AD
Copenhagen establishes its permanent presence with Bishop Absalon's building of a castle on Slotsholmen (see p45).

17th century AD
The reign of Christian IV brings Dutch Renaissance architecture to Copenhagen, visible in the Børsen (see p55), a stock exchange building that dates to 1619-24, and Rosenborg Slot (see p68). Under Christian V, the square of Kongens Nytorv (see p59) is laid out.

1728
A fire destroys most of Copenhagen's wood-built buildings and a third of the medieval city is levelled to the ground. Major rebuilding gets under way.

18th-century
Italian baroque and French rococo combine to produce the extravagant Christiansborg Slot (see p45). Named after the monarch Frederik V (1746-66), Frederiksstaden (see p58) developed as an ambitious planning project for the ruling class, with buildings like Amalienborg Slot (see p65), Marmorkirken (see p65) and what is now Kunstindustrimuseet (see p63) planned during the middle of the century.

Early 19th century
Under the influence of artists like Bertel Thorvaldsen, the first Danish school of painting becomes well established. Danish art flourishes for this is Denmark's Golden Age (1780-1830) and figures as different as Hans Christian Andersen and the philosopher Kirkegaard make their mark.

20th century	The city's architecture is enhanced by the work of Anton Rosen, mostly notably in the *Palace Hotel* edifice and the facade of the *Savoy Hotel*.
1950s	Functionalism, the hallmark of Scandinavian design, reaches maturity in Copenhagen through the work of architects like Arne Jacobsen (see p42).
1990s	Contemporary Danish architecture makes its mark through works like Henning Larsen's gallery in the Ny Carlsberg Glyptotek (see p33), Robert Lund's Arken Museum (see p116), the Black Diamond (see p54) and Terminal 3 at the airport.
2000	The Dansk Design Centre opens in Copenhagen as an exhibition space, conference centre and research and education centre for Danish design.
21st century	A new wave of architecture begins the century with the opening of the Øresund Bridge, soon to be followed by a driverless Metro system, and a brave new world about to unfold in Ørestad, immediately south of the city.

The Vikings

The Vikings – coming from Denmark, Norway and Sweden and spreading through Europe and the North Atlantic in a period of vigorous Scandinavian expansion between around 800 and 1050 – have had a bad press over the centuries.

In Norse, viking means piracy and this is generally how they have been portrayed in history books. In 793 they attacked England's Lindisfarne monastery and two years later began a series of raids along the Irish coast on the lookout for monasteries as a source of booty and slaves. Early chronicles of their activities were written by their victims, the monks, and this naturally skewers accounts of the Vikings. However, they were also traders, entrepreneurs and explorers, and in time began to settle overseas when they found somewhere congenial.

They found amber in the Baltic area as well as skins, furs and walrus tusk ivory in Greenland and these they could trade with merchants in western European towns. They kept open trade routes between the east and west via Byzantium (Constantinople) by way of Kiev and Russia.

Like modern-day Scandinavians, they took a liking to Ireland and founded settlements that developed into the cities of Dublin, Cork, Waterford, Wexford and Limerick. They are credited with making Ireland a centre of western European trade and may have introduced money to the country. In England they made their presence felt in York and helped establish the town as an important trading centre.

The secret of their success lay in their ships. They developed canoe technology to the point that allowed them to venture out from coastlines and into the open sea. With access to the rivers of eastern Europe they could reach the Black Sea and trade with merchants from the Middle East. They are also though to have reached North America some 500 years before Columbus.

Books

Andersen, Hans Christian, *Hans Christian Andersen's Fairy Tales* (1992, Oxford University Press). If you don't dip into them on a trip to Copenhagen, will you ever?

Christensen, Inger, *Alphabet* (2000, Bloodaxe Books). The metaphysics of ordinary life in a slim volume of poetry from one of Denmark's best known writers.

Dyrbye, H, Harris S, Golzen T, *The Xenophobe's Guide to The Danes* (1999, Oval Books). Mildly ironic look at the ways of the Danes.

Høeg Peter, *Miss Smilla's Feeling for Snow* (1993, Harvill Press). A thriller that begins in Copenhagen and ends in Greenland, exploring along the way the colonial and cultural relationship between the two countries.

Høeg Peter, *Tales of the Night* (1998, Harvill Press). Short stories aspiring to a Danish version of magic realism.

Kierkegaard, Søren *Either/or* (1998, Penguin). First published in 1843, this is the most accessible of the philosopher's works.

Strunge, Michael, *A Virgin from a Chilly Decade* (2000, Arc Publications). Committing suicide in 1986, before the age of 30, Strunge's embittered poetry (see p191) runs against the grain of Denmark's putative lightness of being.

Tafdrup, Pia, *Queen's Gate* (2001, Bloodaxe Books). Born in Copenhagen in 1952, Tafdrup received the prestigious 1999 Nordic Council Literature Prize for her ninth collection of poetry.

Language

You don't need Danish to get by but any effort to learn a few words will be rewarded with a smile and a new-found respect.

Greetings, courtesies
Hello *Goddag/Hej (formal/informal)*
Goodbye *Farvel*
Thank you *Tak*

Getting around
Bus *Bussen*
Train *Toget*
Where is...? *Hvor er...?*

Accommodation
Single room *Et enkeltværelse*
Double room *Et dobbeltværelse*
How much is it per night? *Hvor meget koster det per nat?*
How much? *Hvor meget koster?*

Other useful words
Street *Gade*
Old *Gammel*
Garden *Have*
Church *Kirke*
Royal *Kongens*
Little *Lille*
Museum *Museet*
Northern *Nørre*
New *Ny*
Eastern *Øster*
Square *Plads*
Castle *Slot*

Street *Stræde*
Train *Tog*
Square *Torv*

Eating out

Restaurants without a menu in English are fairly uncommon but
even when you are choosing from a Danish menu it is not too
difficult to make out the key terms and, invariably, the waiter is
able to translate.

Bøf Beef
Brød Bread
Is Ice cream
Kaffe (med flød) Coffee (with cream)
Kartofler Potatoes
Kylling Chicken
Laks Salmon
Lam Ham
Osterbord Cheese board
Salat Salad
Sild Herring
Smørrebrød Open sandwich
Storerejer Prawns
Svinekød Pork
Te Tea
Torsk Cod

Smørrebrød

Eaten with a knife and fork, and with never more than one
sandwich on a plate, the open-faced sandwich, *smørrebrød*, means
'butter and bread' and aspires to a form of food art in Denmark.
The ingredients are usually not mixed together but carefully
layered so as to cover every available space on the bread base -
traditionally dark brown or rye bread (pumpernickel is a favourite),
though French white bread or sourdough also works well with

some ingredients. Cover the bread with a generous layer of butter to prevent it becoming soggy and add a piece of lettuce, before proceeding to delicately build up the layers of seafood, meat, egg or cheese.

Here are some suggestions:
Smoked salmon, followed by scrambled egg, then cucumber, and garnished with asparagus tips or dill.
Slices of hard-boiled egg, followed by strips of crisp bacon, topped with tomato, anchovies as an optional extra, topped with fresh parsley.
Slices of roast beef, garnished with horseradish.
Ham, followed by scrambled egg, asparagus, tomato, and parsley for garnish.
Strips of cheese, followed by rows of shrimp, dips of mayonnaise, decorated with sprigs of parsley.

Herring salad

If you really want to go Danish, try this herring salad

Dice and mix together a small amount of cooked meat, cold potatoes, flour, beetroot, onion, butter, mustard and smoked or pickled herring. Add some vinegar to help make the mix stick together, and also a sprinkling of sugar if you wish. Spread the salad over the bread, and add some slices of hard boiled egg to give the dish some colour.

Index

Credits

Footprint credits

Text editor: Stephanie Lambe
Series editor: Rachel Fielding

Production: Jo Morgan, Mark Thomas
Davina Rungasamy
In-house cartography: Claire Benison,
Kevin Feeney, Robert Lunn,
Sarah Sorensen
Proof-reading: Elizabeth Barrick

Design: Mytton Williams
Maps: PCGraphics (UK) Ltd

Photography credits

Front cover: Olivier Cirendini,
Lonely Planet images
Inside: Julius Honnor
Generic images: John Matchett
Back cover: Julius Honnor

Print

Manufactured in Italy by LegoPrint

Publishing information

Footprint Copenhagen
1st edition
Text and maps © Footprint Handbooks
Ltd March 2003

ISBN 1 903471 58 3
CIP DATA: a catalogue record for this
book is available from the British Library

® Footprint Handbooks and the Footprint
mark are a registered trademark of
Footprint Handbooks Ltd

Published by Footprint Handbooks
6 Riverside Court
Lower Bristol Road
Bath, BA2 3DZ, UK
T +44 (0)1225 469141
F +44 (0)1225 469461
E discover@footprintbooks.com
W www.footprintbooks.com

Distributed in the USA by
Publishers Group West

Every effort has been made to ensure
that the facts in this pocket Handbook
are accurate. However the authors and
publishers cannot accept responsibility
for any loss, injury or inconvenience
sustained by any traveller as a result of
information or advice contained in this
guide.

Complete title list

(P) denotes pocket
Handbook

Publishing stuff

For a different view…
choose a Footprint

Over 80 Footprint travel guides
Covering more than 145 of the world's most exciting
countries and cities in Latin America, the Caribbean, Africa, Indian
sub-continent, Australasia, North America, Southeast Asia, the
Middle East and Europe.

Discover so much more…
The finest writers. In-depth knowledge. Entertaining and accessible.
Critical restaurant and hotels reviews. Lively descriptions of all the
attractions. Get away from the crowds.

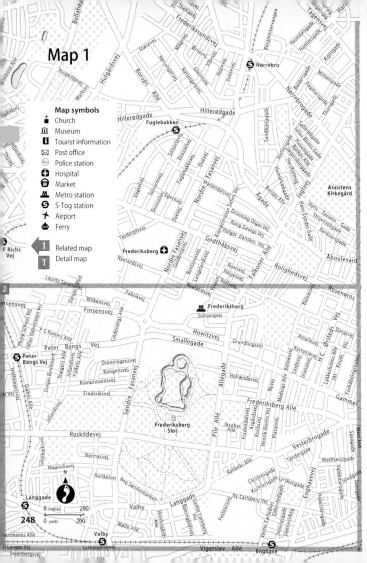

Map 1

Map symbols

✚	Church
🏛	Museum
ℹ	Tourist information
✉	Post office
(Pol)	Police station
🏥	Hospital
M	Market
Ⓜ	Metro station
S	S-Tog station
✈	Airport
⛴	Ferry

1 Related map

1 Detail map

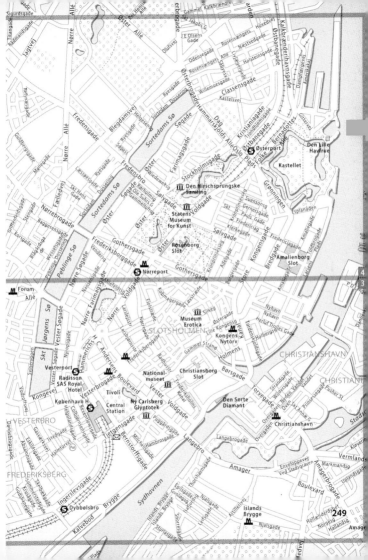

249

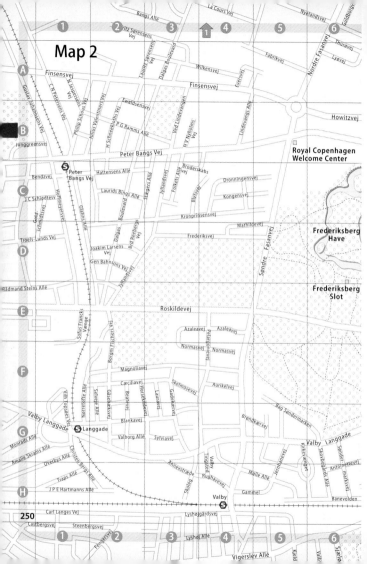

Map 2

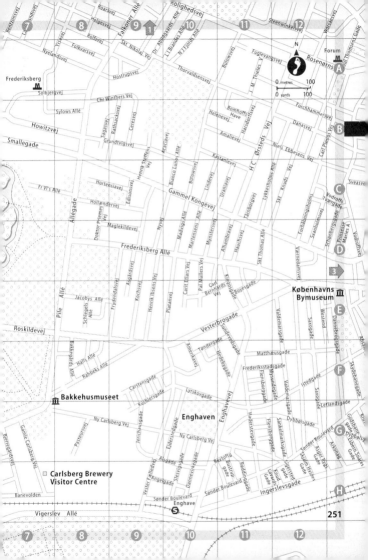

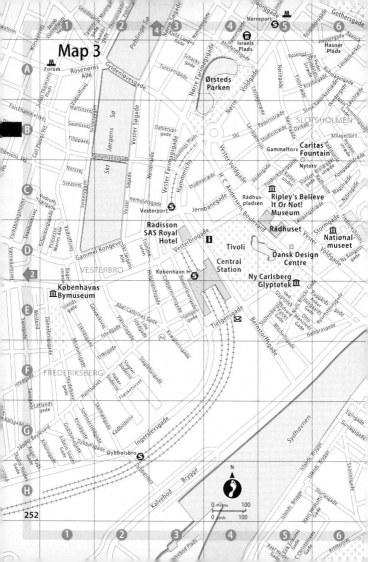

Map 3

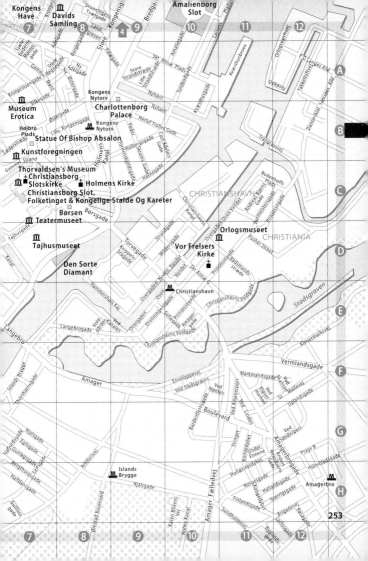

Kongens Have
Davids Samling
7
8
Amalienborg Slot
10
11
12
4
9

Sølvgade

Kronprinsensgade
Silkegade
Museum Erotica
Højbro Plads
Kunstforeningen

Statue Of Bishop Absalon

Thorvaldsen's Museum
Christiansborg
Slotskirke
Holmens Kirke
Christiansborg Slot,
Folketinget & Kongelige Stalde Og Kareter
Børsen
Teatermuseet

Tøjhusmuseet

Den Sorte
Diamant

Langebro

Kongens Nytorv
Charlottenborg
Palace
Kongens Nytorv

Nyhavn

CHRISTIANSHAVN

Orlogsmuseet
CHRISTIANIA

Vor Frelsers
Kirke

Christianshavn

Stadsgraven

Vermlandsgade

Amager

Islands
Brygge

Ved Stadsgraven

Amagerbro Boulevard

Amagerbro

7
8
9
10
11
12

A
B
C
D
E
F
G
H

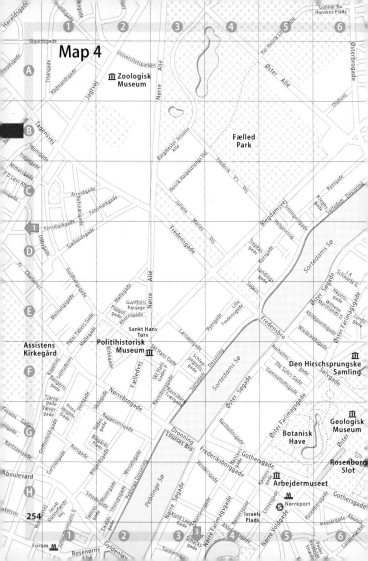

Map 4

Gunnar Nu Hansens Plads

Haraldsgade

Sigurdsgade

Universitetsparken

🏛 Zoologisk Museum

Fælled Park

Titangade

Rådmandsgade

Jagtvej

Tagensvej

Ydungade

Frejasgade

Mimersgade

P.D Løvs Allé

Arresøgade

Refnæsgade

Fensmarkgade

Sjællandsgade

Fensmarkgade

Charlottes

Guldbergsgade

Meinungsgade

Peter Fabers Gade

Møllegade

Mallegade

Gunthers Passage

Poppel gade

Sankt Hans Torv

🏛 Politihistorisk Museum

Assistens Kirkegård

Kapelvej

Solitudevej

Rantzausgade

Prins Jørgens Gade

Jægersborggade

Stefansgade

Fælledvej

Nørrebrogade

Birkegade

Skt Hans Gade

Sankt Hans Gade

Ravnsborggade

Ravnsborg Tværgade

Schleppegrelsgade

Dosseringen

Sortedam Dossering

Den Hirschsprungske Samling

🏛

Griffenfeldtsgade

Korsgade

Baggesensgade

Blågårds Plads

Wesselsgade

Dronning Louises Bro

Peblinge Sø

Nørre Søgade

Frederiksborggade

Vendersgade

Gothersgade

Øster Farimagsgade

Botanisk Have

Geologisk Museum

Rosenborg Slot

🏛 Arbejdermuseet

Ⓢ Nørreport

Aboulevard

Nørre Søgade

Nørre Farimagsgade

Nørre Voldgade

Israels Plads

Ahlefeldtsgade

Forum Ⓜ

Rosenørns

Gyldenløv

Turesensgade